OVERCOMING MEDIOCRITY

COURAGEOUS WOMEN

OVERCOMING *Mediocrity*©

**A unique collection of stories from courageous women
who have created their own lives of significance!**

Presented by Christie L. Ruffino

DPWN Publishing

www.overcomingmediocrityteam.com

For more information, contact:
DPWN Publishing
A division of the Dynamic Professional Women's Network, Inc.
1879 N. Neltnor Blvd. #316, West Chicago, IL 60185
www.overcomingmediocrityteam.com
www.dpwomen.com

Printed in the United States of America

ISBN: 978-1-939794-00-0

Dedication

To every woman who does not believe she can make a difference and to every woman who believes she can move a mountain.

To every woman who continually makes sacrifices for those she loves and to every woman who prioritizes those moments when she can pamper and take care of her own needs.

To every woman who believes that she should settle for the life she has and to every woman who has overcome great odds to create her own life of significance.

To the courageous women in this book who have shared their stories with you in hopes that their lessons of pain will become your lessons of power.

To the women in my life who believe I am significant and whom I believe are priceless.

The Power of Story

The best speakers are good storytellers. The best leaders are good storytellers. The best teachers, coaches and trainers are good storytellers. And I am certain that the best writers are always good storytellers.

While storytelling is not the only way to engage people with your ideas, it is certainly a critical part of the recipe because stories are powerful and memorable and they personalize the message being shared.

The right story can alter the course of someone's life just by hearing it.

But, the most powerful aspect of stories is that if you can change the direction of the story you are living, you can change your destiny.

Introduction

Welcome to our second in a series of anthology books that are intended to provide women with a platform to share their stories of encouragement, inspiration and prosperity. Our first book, Overcoming Mediocrity - Dynamic Edition, was a smashing success and was released on May of 2013 with 22 participating authors sharing their stories. Plus we achieved bestselling status on Amazon in the motivational genre category in only one day. Yeah!!!!

My goal with this project initially was to provide the women of my organization, The Dynamic Professional Women's Network, Inc., a platform to share their stories and then leverage their new author status to gain additional exposure for their business. However, it ended up taking on a life of its own and it made a bigger impact than anticipated as I started to hear testimonials from women who read the book and connected with one or more of the inspirational stories inside.

Because of this initial overwhelming success, I decided to develop a new vision for this venture which is much larger than the previous one. My new "Exciting, Magical and Wildly Epic Goal" for this project is to build the Overcoming Mediocrity brand stronger and to have our collection of books become nationally recognized and carried by the big book stores in addition to our current Amazon distribution. I want the authors of the current, past and future volumes to gain increased exposure and greater blessings for aligning themselves with this project so they can share their stories with larger audiences and make a greater impact. (The Chicken Soup series did it, why can't we?)

It is with great honor and pride that I am able to share with you the stories from the courageous women on the following pages of this book, which is the second anthology book in this series. I have had the pleasure of getting to know each of these ladies to learn a little about whom they are and about the courageous stories they planned to share. I am also deeply inspired by the courage that they are still exhibiting by sharing some personal details of their lives with the sole intention of equipping the reader to learn from their experiences and to spare themselves a little pain, if possible. Not only does this demonstrate courage, but humility and the heart of a true go-giver. These women, while still on the amazing journey of their lives, all have great things yet to come. They are women who you should know, learn from and emulate.

I am blessed to have had that opportunity.

Christie

Table of Contents

Christie Ruffino

Permission to be Imperfect

Why do we, so often, compare and judge ourselves to other people who we "think" have it all together? Why do we, way too often, get down on ourselves when we don't look a certain way or have certain abilities that we admire in others? We can set up such high expectations for ourselves and base our happiness by peering through a looking glass and comparing our world to the seemingly perfect world of others.

What is Perfection, really?

Whether we are making assumptions about that perfect looking person that we see walk by us on the street, or assume that the poised looking person on the cover of Success Magazine is happy because they have enough money to buy all of their heart's desires. Or when someone we know is continually bragging about themselves and the things that they have, we have to recognize that our perception of them may not even be their reality nor is it even ours.

When we were children, untarnished by the fiscal and social responsibilities of adulthood, our lives were much simpler and more joyful. Then we grew up and life became so very complicated. And if you are anything like me, we can be the major contributor to our own complicatedness because of our unrealistic need to be perfect. But you know as well as I do, that the world is anything but perfect. We are not perfect. And those perfect looking people we see every day are really perfectly imperfect people in deep disguise.

I have permission to be imperfect.

Part of my journey this last year, while trying to keep up with my continually evolving networking organization, The Dynamic Professional Women's Network, Inc. www.dpwomen.com, was to identify my own personal purpose, mission and brand. Although I love managing an organization that helps women have the right resources they need to be successful in their businesses, I needed to make sure that I was not losing myself and my needs in the process. I realized that I wanted to do more than process members and coach leaders. I have learned so much about how to market and run a successful business during this journey that I wanted to get back to helping my members on a more one-on-one basis to create their own distinct and memorable brand. I also wanted to help them create their own personal websites and utilize social media and other internet tools to help them acquire and manage new customers.

Most people underutilize their professional expertise and waste the opportunity for sharing that knowledge and helping more people. They are motivated by serving and not by money so they don't follow opportunities to capitalize on sharing their knowledge because they think it is self-serving and not others-serving. But how do you feel when you meet someone or hear someone speak who has knowledge that fascinates you and inspires you to learn more? Wouldn't you like to be able to perform the Vulcan mind-meld to merge the essence of that person's mind into yours? Absolutely!

Do you know Sara and Jim?

Sara is a good friend of mine who, because of her child's health issues, has become an expert in the field of nutrition, specifically about whole food wellness. She has learned how eating whole organic fruits and vegetables can not only make us healthier, but could also cure and prevent diseases. She has enough knowledge in her head to write a whole library of books about this subject and could speak to an audience of thousands and provide them with valuable resources and knowledge to make informed decisions about their future dietary consumption. We know that there is a whole slew of information out there about this subject, but the abundance of information only makes it more difficult for us to research it all, discern the truth and what is not so we can utilize what we need to and discard the rest. Sara already knows it all. She has done the research to help guide us through everything from reading labels to whole food nutrition. Her knowledge can empower us to live healthier, longer and more pain free lives as well as can save us money on healthcare costs, but does she share this knowledge? She only shares it to her few personal training clients.

Jim on the other hand, claims to have found the cure for genital warts. I am not saying that he has nor has not because I cannot give a personal testimonial about his product, but I do know that he has created a very successful business marketing the opportunity to buy his knowledge. He has created a very simple website that outlines the benefits you will receive by trying his product. He has created a one-click ordering process and he is marketing the heck out of his business. He has over the past years earned a significant amount of revenue by sharing this secret cure that allows him to live a very luxurious life and he has claimed to help thousands of people rid themselves of this embarrassing disease.

I know that Sara and Jim's stories seem to be two of very opposite extremes, but I am sure you can relate to both of them in one way or another. We all have knowledge worth sharing and we all want to be able to enjoy the luxuries of life. Are you doing anything about it like Jim did? Or are you more like Sara?

My goal is to help direct my members down the right path to create their own learning webinars or informational products to share or sell to their current or potential clients. These are products that will offer value and establish their expertise in a duplicable manner that will let them help more than one person at a time.

If only the stars would align.

One of the challenges that I faced during my journey this past year to define my personal purpose, mission and brand, is that the stars would just not align to allow me the time and opportunity to focus solely on figuring out a plan to execute these goals. I still had chapters to manage, leaders to support, a book to launch and market, another book to start and interview authors for, a house to maintain, kids to help, dogs to feed, etc., etc., etc. Life was just getting in the way. But one thing I kept reminding myself of was a clever little lesson I learned from Lisa Sasevich, The Queen of Sales Conversion, on how we can "build the plane as we're flying it". We all know that in reality this statement is the farthest from the truth as a work in progress statement, but it resonated with me probably because of that reason. Why do we feel that we have to wait until everything is in order before we can proceed? I know I have, but with Lisa's help, I have given myself permission to be "imperfect"

You should try it!

And now since I have permission to make mistakes, perform below par and be incomplete, I have no more excuses to delay the launch of my new brand and ever evolving personal website. I have no more excuses to delay supporting women by sharing my knowledge in a new weekly "This Week I Learned" blog post that will include weekly rants in addition to informational training videos on relevant business topics. (I have been posting daily "Today I Learned" quotes for two years now) In addition, this year will be the beginning of many new changes for me including many new improvements for my tribe of professional women who are members of the Dynamic Professional Women's Network, Inc. (www.dpwomen.com), including a new website makeover, another Overcoming Mediocrity volume, yearly leadership retreats and my first ever national Dynamic Women's Conference.

I welcome you to join me on this journey and I encourage you to take a peek at my new christieruffino.com website. It is not perfect yet, but it is on its way. And if you can give yourself permission to be imperfect too, you can start a new amazing imperfect journey of your own.

Please invite me along.

Hugs! CR

Christie Ruffino

Christie Ruffino is the President and Founder of the Dynamic Professional Women's Network, Inc., which is an industry exclusive networking organization designed to help women create partnerships with each other to generate ideas, alliances, and revenues within a structured referral generating format.

Five years since its conception, more than 1400 members have joined DPWN, recognizing it as a driving force behind the success and profitability for many of its members' businesses. In addition to working diligently to ensure the success of the Dynamic Professional Women's Network, the DPWN Angel Foundation and the new DPWN Publishing, Ms. Ruffino has served as a Council Member of the Executives Breakfast Club, she served two terms as a Board Director of the Carol Stream Chamber of Commerce, she was honored to receive a Special Judge's Recognition for the Citizen of the year award in Carol Stream, was awarded a Distinguished Woman of Business

Award from American Family Insurance and received her highest honors by being recognized as an Influential Women in Business in 2009 by the Business Ledger and the National Association of Women Business Owners (NAWBO) and in 2010 with an Entrepreneurial Excellence Award.

Christie L. Ruffino
info@christieruffino.com
www.christieruffino.com

Dynamic Professional Women's Network, Inc.
1879 N. Neltnor Blvd. #316
West Chicago, IL 60185
630-336-3773
info@dpwomen.com
www.dpwomen.com

Giana Ferrari

Perceptions

Dear Woman from the Grocery Store,

You are incorrect: I should not be ashamed of myself.

I imagine that, aside from your personal victory, today was like any ordinary day for you. You woke up, drove the kids to school and began to tackle your daily to-do list. On the list: go to the grocery store to buy food for you and your family.

Today, however, was different. Today you had the chance to act superior and judge someone for a necessary action they took in order to get through their day the same way you were trying to get through yours.

After you parked your minivan, you saw something that made you angry.

You saw me.

You saw a seemingly healthy, brunette-haired girl, just shy of twenty years old, use a handicapped parking pass. You saw me place my state-issued parking permit on the front windshield of my car. You saw me walk into the grocery store with ease.

You became furious.

You may have become furious because you have a child with a physical disability. Or perhaps you have a friend or relative who uses a wheelchair to get around. You most likely know someone who you believe truly relies on that handicapped permit.

Someone like me.

Your immediate reaction was to follow me around the grocery store to see how I handled myself. You may have noticed that I didn't travel very far. I gathered just a few items in my shopping basket to bring home to my family.

Your anger grew stronger and stronger until you couldn't take it anymore. You finally tapped me on the shoulder. The words you spoke I will never forget.

"Excuse me, dear. Let me carry your basket since you're handicapped and all. You really should be ashamed of yourself."

Your tone was perfectly sarcastic. Everyone who saw the incident could feel the pride radiating from you. They became proud of you, too.

I was shaken but not broken. It took me a few seconds to gather the courage to tap you on the shoulder to return the favor.

"Excuse me, Miss. I know you mean well but I had heart surgery two weeks ago. I am not supposed to walk far distances." I continued, "Just because I don't look like I have a disability doesn't mean that it isn't there."

My tone was quiet and my voice was shaky. I exhibited about a tenth of the confidence that you showed.

What you didn't know was that I also had a small victory today. It was the first time I could drive all by myself following my pacemaker surgery. A veteran of over twenty heart surgeries and procedures, this operation, typically a life-changing event for most people, was simply routine for me.

You also didn't know that I was born with skin color as blue as the sea. The lack of oxygen I had at birth signaled the doctors that I had a congenital heart condition. I endured open heart surgery before I could speak in complete sentences. I requested the butterfly needle as a toddler. I relied on a pacemaker since the age of nine.

I gave you a snapshot of my physical wounds as I showed you my fresh 6-inch scar just below my right shoulder. It was still covered in Steri-Strip bandages to prevent infection.

I could see tears welling up in your eyes. My intention was not to make you upset. My intention was to inform you.

I hope you went home today feeling just that—informed.

Miss, I urge you to tell your friends, family and everyone you know about the experience that we shared today.

I wish I could tell you that this was the first time I was judged in this type of situation. I wish I could tell you that this will be the last. But it won't be.

Unfortunately, I am not alone. There are so many people like me. People who deal with aches, pains and anxiety on a daily basis. People who have debilitating chronic conditions that are invisible to strangers who see how apparently healthy we look.

Thank you, stranger at the grocery store, for what you did today. You made my confidence a little bit stronger.

Now all I need is my heart to follow suit.

Sincerely,

Giana

Giana Ferrari

As someone who's grown up with an invisible disability, Giana feels that it is her calling to help those in a similar situation achieve independence and understanding in their daily lives.

Giana Ferrari is the founder of Ferrari Resource Group, LLC. Her business provides client-centered services for young adults with disabilities and their families through advocacy, vocational counseling and job coaching.

Giana also works as an Accommodations Specialist for students with disabilities in the Center of Access and Accommodations at College of DuPage.

Giana received her undergraduate degree in business management, entrepreneurship and psychology from Elmhurst College. She received her graduate degree in rehabilitation counseling at Northern Illinois University.

In her free time, Giana volunteers as a spokesperson for the American

Heart Association. She also enjoys training her dog Calvin, and spending time with her family, including her loving husband Brandon Ayers.

Giana Ferrari, M.A., CRC

Ferrari Resource Group, LLC

giana.ferrari@gmail.com

www.gianaferrari.com

Michele Malo

Redefining Success

I am a certified personal trainer (CPT). That statement has been years in the making, not only from the standpoint of the training and studying it takes to become a CPT but also from a mental standpoint. Who I am today is my true authentic self. I found my true north; but it was quite a journey to get here, and to get here I needed to redefine success.

My story begins with a happy and loving childhood that just happened to have a divorce thrown into the mix. My dad left our little family when I was four years old. As terrible as that sounds, the experience truly molded, good and bad, the person that I am today. It also was the moment when I began to define success and my happiness based on things that I cannot control which are all external factors – in particular, people.

My mom always said, "It is us against the world." To this day, this statement still holds true as she is my best friend and someone who is a rock in my life. She went back to work and that's when a lot of angels came in to help our little family unit. My grandparents, Dot and Robert, were like a second set of parents to me, and still are everything to me. My great grandparents also stepped in, moving two blocks away to take care of me when my mom went back to work to support our family. I miss them all tons. Yes, I am blessed to have known and been loved by three generations.

Don't count my dad out. He was a very active part of my life and I love him very much. He was in sales, and it gave him the opportunity to be at my softball games, to take me to and participate in Girl Scout events and to be a field trip dad. He remarried and had two sons, and even though that was hard for me in the beginning, I am grateful to have two brothers in my life. I have two families, so to speak.

That is a bit of the back story. It was nothing really traumatic. I was surrounded by people who loved and cared for me.

So what does this have to do with life transformation and defining success?

At some point – I am not sure if it was because of a fear of people leaving me – I became a people pleaser. Not just a little, but a lot. All I wanted was for the people in my life to be proud of me and I wanted – no, I *needed* – people to give me accolades. This started when I was in school. I wanted to be the student of the day. If I did not ace my tests, I would feel bad and embarrassed to show my mom my report card.

In the first grade, I broke my arm at the school skating party. A stupid eighth-grader took me out. My dad was there (I told you that he did a lot of the school events) and, yep, my right wrist was broken. They put a cast on and then it was time to go back to school. In the first grade you practice writing and I remember getting a C because I had to write with my non-dominant hand. It shouldn't have been a big deal. It was a handwriting grade and I had an excuse, but I was devastated. I remember crying because my report card had this ugly grade on it. My mom tried to talk me off the ledge, but I took it personally. That began the pattern of needing to be perfect. Even though the rest of my grades were stellar, all I saw was the one flaw.

This carried over to my relationships with friends in school. Anyone who knows me now is not sure how this was possible, but I was a doormat. Most of my friends were the dominant ones and the ones that you followed. I was not a leader. I was the follower. If someone did not like me, I was relentless at bowing down until I could turn them around so that they could see how awesome I was. I was the really nice one. I was again defining myself by how many people liked me.

A big part of my story involves self-esteem. My weight started to be an issue when I was young. It began in about the third grade, and got worse as I approached those awkward preteen years. I was heavy (I mean really heavy), had braces and was the dork in school. For someone who defines success by other people's thoughts and actions, this was hard. Kids are mean, especially boys at that age. They teased me relentlessly.

I did have some amazing friends. Mary, Anne and Mo were my neighbors who lived two houses down. They went to a different school and were not able to buffer me during the day. However, to this day they are my best friends. They never judged me or made me feel bad. They were just the real deal.

So why did I put so much emphasis on the negative instead of the joy that I had in some great friends and an amazing family? I am still trying to figure that one out, but this pattern has continued throughout my adult life.

Let's fast forward: I broke out of my shell in high school. I did slim down to 5'6" and 135 pounds, but I still saw the fat girl, looking back at me.

The next step was college. I started at DePaul and all was good. I joined the Alpha Sigma Alpha sorority. Some of those girls are still in my life today. There was a lot of lady bug love (it's a sorority thing). All was good, but then I decided to follow one of my sorority sisters to Nebraska. (See the pattern here? I *followed*.) She was a cool party friend. I use the term "friend" very loosely. Everything was fine until I started to branch out and meet people in school. She was jealous and proceeded to make my life miserable. She was my roommate and tried to turn the friends I had made against me. She succeeded. She was very persuasive and a big liar. However, as I talked about earlier, I defined my success and self-esteem by others' thoughts and actions. As a result, I felt alone and miserable. I was in Nebraska living with a psycho!

It was during college when I really started to pile on the weight. There were many late nights out partying and 2am Amigos runs (cheap Mexican food, for you non-Nebraskans). This did not help my health and well-being.

As always, angels came into my life: Jenn, Heather and Shelley. It was then that I realized that people who are toxic need to go. My attention needs to be in the present with those who add joy and love to my life.

I finished college in the top 10% of my class, with a degree in advertising and marketing. My goal was to be the top in my field. I wanted to run a corporate marketing department. I have always felt the need to be the best. It is rooted in teachings from my mom who told me to "never depend on anyone but yourself for your well-being." I took this to heart. But there I was, living in my mom's basement with no car, no money and no idea what I was going to do. I was depressed and finding solace in food.

I began my job search and found myself with a temp agency that placed me at a very popular donut chain's Chicago office as an operations assistant. I took this job and ran with it. I hope that by showing them what I could do it might lead to a marketing opportunity. And it did: I worked and worked, getting promotions with more responsibility. With each promotion I felt better, but I was in a financial hole after finishing college. I was constantly dodging bill collectors and just getting by. The food I ate was very unhealthy. I was feeding my stress and, honestly, it was cheaper to run through a drive thru than to buy groceries (which I now know is not true). I could have paid a manager's salary at many fast food places for how often I picked up food there.

This is where you can start to see the pattern develop for the rest of my eighteen-year corporate career. I threw myself into my work by working 12-14 hour days. I was always on call, weekends and holidays. I did whatever the job required or I thought it required. I was always stressed, always working and always eating. Exercise was nothing but a passing idea that I would throw money at after watching infomercials on TV.

As my career progressed, I never felt like I was good enough. I was always comparing myself to others. I looked at where they were and compared it to where I was in my career. I was always trying to do more to get ahead. I decided to pursue an MBA with an international specialization. If I had no time before, I had now just added in a master's program. Needless to say, my weight continued to climb. I was now at about 250 pounds which was not going to be the top number.

During this time I met a wonderful man (my husband Jim). He was extremely supportive and very blunt. I always knew what he was thinking. It was good for me, but also bad because I am so damn sensitive. He met me at 250 pounds and loved me for who I was. He was another angel in my life. It was time to start believing in myself – but not just yet.

My career continued on the upswing as I took various positions within many of the largest Chicago based food manufacturing companies. But, as my career continued to climb, so did my weight; reaching an all-time high of 310 pounds.

When you work in the food service industry and manage top convenience food brands, you are surrounded by food. As much as I love those brands, they are not on the healthy side of the spectrum. It was like an alcoholic working for a beer company. I was a food addict working with food all day long. I was struggling mightily. My weight and stress levels were at their all-time highs. My health was deteriorating. I was one of the sickest 28-year-olds that you would ever meet.

A decision needed to be made. I had had my gallbladder removed a few years earlier, but now I was hypertensive, pre-diabetic, had a heart murmur and my knees and back could hardly support my weight. I would wake up and just getting out of bed would throw my back out for three days. But I was successful. I had that great job, a fiancé, a home and almost an MBA.

It was time to redefine my reality. After talking it over with my fiancé, Jim, I decided that I needed to take control and had gastric bypass surgery. It worked: I dropped almost 150 pounds. This was life changing, but I was ashamed that I had to resort to surgery in order to undo the damage that I had done to my body and self-esteem.

I finished my MBA in May of 2003 and was married in October of that same year. I was feeling accomplished, successful and my career was full steam ahead. But my outside success did not portray how I felt inside. What the surgery did not fix was my lifestyle or how I saw myself.

I held my weight pretty steady for a few years. However, I was still my worst critic. Every time I looked in the mirror, I still saw the fat girl and viewed the hanging skin as a reminder of what I did to myself. The negative self-talk was brutal. As they say, what you believe will become your reality, and so it began.

It began slowly, a pound here, five there, but because my self-image was already so tarnished I was fulfilling what I saw in the mirror. The weight started to come back on. I was now a marketing executive and was traveling all over the world. I had finally made it…but I was miserable.

I was always still comparing myself to others. Even when I received accolades or promotions (which I needed to feel successful), it was not enough. I dreaded performance reviews. Even constructive criticism was associated in my mind with failure.

I continued to throw myself into my work. When I began work for the Italian pasta company it really began to go downhill. I was traveling all the time and I was a one-woman band. I felt like the success of the department rode on my shoulders because of my horrible manager, who was let go for various ugly reasons. However, it took over a year for that to happen. I felt like I was at rock bottom. I was not happy. I was back up to 220 pounds.

I threw money at the problem by spending it on shopping, personal trainers, etc. I actually had about 20 pairs of black Chico's pants. But that would only give me momentary happiness. I had no spontaneity in my life. I was scheduled out a year in advance. My friends continued to invite me out, but they were guessing where I was in the world. Thank God that I have those angels; they didn't give up on me. Thanks, Cindy, MP, Therese, Katie, Dawn and Mindi.

As you know, marriage needs work and I was not putting anything into it. When you are unhappy you take it out on the people closest to you and that was my husband Jim. I knew I had to make a change not only for my health but for my relationships and my overall sanity.

One night at the bar, I said to my husband, I have an idea. He raised his eyebrows and asked if he should order another drink; I said probably. I talked to him about leaving corporate America and going back to school to become a personal trainer. I wanted to be able to take control of my own health, and doing it under the stress of corporate politics with food controlling my life did not seem like a viable option. Could we give up my salary? Would he support this drastic move that was giving up a career I nearly killed myself trying to achieve?

What was his response? "I never said you had to be CMO (chief marketing officer). I just want to grow old with you." Wow.

We made a plan for me to leave my job and to start personal training school at NPTI. My nerves were on full throttle as I walked into school again at 38-years old and 220 pounds, to be a personal trainer. Was I crazy? All I kept thinking was that everyone was going to be fit and young. It was like I was in grammar school all over again. I was very afraid of being judged and not included.

This was not the case. I have never felt more welcomed in my life. It was weird because my classmates actually thought that my story was cool and even inspiring. They did not judge me when I could not do certain exercises. They helped me and encouraged me. They were my biggest cheerleaders and for that I thank them.

During school (I am a bit competitive, especially with myself) I did what I always do and pushed myself to the limits. What happened? I tore my rotator cuff which required complete reconstructive shoulder surgery. If you can ever avoid shoulder surgery, please do. It was the most painful physical event I have ever gone through. What a setback. I was losing weight, getting stronger and bam, reality hit me hard, really hard. All the self-doubt came back. I felt like I had failed.

However, this time was different. I didn't give up and I didn't go back to corporate America. Instead, I strapped on my sling and finished. I was a little worse for wear, but finished. I took the time while rehabbing and set up a business, Wellcome Home, LLC. It's clever, huh? You would think that I had been in marketing. The idea was to do in-home personal training, focusing on people who needed help with weight loss. It was not just weight loss. It required someone who understood what it meant to struggle with your self-image and esteem. Weight loss can be 10 pounds or 100 pounds. It doesn't matter if you are not comfortable within your own skin.

I removed the fear of the gym and the fear of being judged. This allowed my clients to focus on the task at hand which is living a healthier lifestyle.

I was on my way, sort of.

It is necessary to go back to how I defined success. As I set up my business, my savings had dwindled because the shoulder injury threw my business plan months behind. Now I was JUST a personal trainer.

Let me explain "just a personal trainer." For years, I always defined my life and happiness levels by external success factors such as grades, awards, degrees, corporate positions and how others saw me. As I went to different networking events, joined the chamber of commerce and DPWN, people asked what I did for a living. I felt that saying I was a personal trainer was not good enough. I always felt like I needed to explain my story, or give my elevator speech, so they knew that I was more.

In came my elevator speech: "I left corporate America and 160 pounds behind so you can live a healthier lifestyle." Good, right? It made people go, wow, 160 pounds, how did you do that?

Here is a funny twist to the story. For years I was embarrassed to let folks know that I had gastric bypass surgery. I was afraid that it took away from the work I did. I was afraid that people would think less of the accomplishment because I had "the surgery." My success was not as big of a deal because I "cheated." I knew how much work it was, but I was so concerned about what others thought. I felt like I had to talk it down and to emphasize diet and exercise. It was not a lie, but not really the whole truth either.

It was not until I lost the weight the last time that I became proud of my journey. I cannot even tell you how many business/self-help books I owned and Oprah shows I watched over the years to help fix myself and become happy. I knew that I began to heal when I went to my book shelves and purged the self-help books. I had so many of them that the Goodwill folks looked at me sideways. It took me a little longer to get over Oprah. I remember having lunch with a good friend and telling her that I cancelled my magazine subscription and email alerts from Oprah because I had decided I did not need fixing, I just needed to start believing. That was a breakthrough for me.

The next breakthrough came when I finally started to listen to my friend Michele. She has been like a guardian angel and a confidante with my weight and self-image. She always told me to know who I am and to wear clothes that fit. She told me not to hide from the world under your clothes. We joked that the *What Not to Wear* team was probably following me around, recording secret footage. I finally took her advice. I went into my closet and took anything over a size 10 to a consignment shop. It amounted to four lawn bags' worth of name brand work clothes. As I saw my "success" spread all over the floor, separated into keep and donate piles, I started to have a panic attack. First, I was counting how much money I had spent and how I had tried to find happiness in stuff. Second, for years those clothes were my identity as a marketing executive. This was the last step in giving it up for gym shoes and yoga pants. At that moment, it was not about weight loss. It was about the regret that I allowed myself to be unhappy for so many years, when I had so many reasons not to be.

That was a turning point for me. Don't get me wrong, I do miss the paychecks from time to time and self-doubt seems to creep in when I am not on guard. But my business is growing and my life coach Melissa helps me to see the simplicity of my life. When you don't make assumptions and control only what you can change, good things will come into your life. You have to be ready to accept in order for the right things to happen. The time will come.

You just need to be patient.

My business has started to turn the corner. It is not even about how many personal training clients I have or how many people want to buy Juice Plus or Usana from me. It is about how many people I have inspired to be better today than yesterday, which is now how I am defining my success.

Here are some things I learned on this journey:

1) Be happy with where you are in the current moment.

    a. Don't wait to do things that make you happy until… (insert wish here).

2) Make a plan that you embrace; not something everyone else thinks *should* be your plan.

    a. You want to get in shape, so you decide to run 5 miles every day…*but you HATE running.*

    b. You want to run the company, that is the logical progression… *but you already feel stressed and pressured and are unhappy with the lack of family time.*

    c. Kids are not in your plan even though that's the next logical step…*then don't have them.*

3) Keep expectations in check:

    a. Make sure that your timeline is realistic.

    b. Make sure that you dream, but have a plan and stepping stones in place to get there.

    c. Be nice to yourself; if a goal is not met, reassess and restructure.

4) You are you. Do not define yourself by your job title or relationships.

5) Always remember that without your health all other plans get put on hold.

6) Reassess your relationship with time. That way, what you prioritize gets done.

This journey for me has just begun and I cannot adequately thank the people in my life, my angels who constantly remind me how blessed a life I have. I have the opportunity to work with friends every day and help them and myself to live our best lives.

Today when I'm asked what I do, I say I am the owner of Wellcome Home Fitness. I am a personal trainer.

The end.

Success.

Michele Malo

I am the owner of Wellcome Home, LLC and an Advanced Certified Personal Trainer. I left corporate America and 160 lbs behind to help you live a healthier lifestyle. I worked 18 years for food service manufacturers such as Kraft, Kellogg and Barilla and with thousands of airline miles to my credit decided to pack it up, and utilize my MBA for my own business.

Almost 10 years ago, I had gastric bypass surgery only to find my weight creep back up with all the stress and travel associated with my career. I understand what it means to battle your weight and it is my dream to help others take back control of their lives. Making small changes when put together make a big difference. I can help you with your journey by offering in-home personal and small group training. Here is the journey I undertook to be qualified to help you.

Certified Personal Training certification, National Personal Training Institute;

100 hours in nutrition education, NPTI;

Certified Personal Trainer certification, National Academy of Sports Medicine; Myofascial Compression Techniques Specialization, Trigger Point Performance Therapy;

CPR/AED certified, American Heart Association; Fitness Boot Camp Specialty, SCW; Hip Hop Hustle Instructor, Powder Blue Productions/Beach body;

Kick Boxing Certified Instructor, IFTA.

I am also a Juice Plus, Usana and Beach body coach to help you enhance your nutrition options, with fruits, vegetables and protein.

Michele Malo, CPT, MBA

Wellcome Home, LLC
116 E. Hawthorne
Arlington Heights, IL 60004
847-951-1189
wellcomehome14@gmail.com
www.wc-h.com

Deborah McPhee

Choices

The choices we make shape our lives, and we have to live with them, whatever they may be. Some people are like merry-go-rounds. They make solid, no risk choices and live their lives going round and round, within the boundaries of safety. Other people are like roller coasters. They take risks. Their highs are high and their lows are low. I am a risk-taker. I never regret anything because at one point, it was exactly what I wanted. I am in a good place in my life right now and I know I would never have gotten here without the choices I made, even the bad ones.

I grew up in the southwest corner of Chicago, St Thomas More Parish. In Chicago, it is perfectly acceptable to answer your parish name instead of your street location when anyone asks where you lived. My parents were the first "divorced" people in the entire neighborhood. My mother had an important choice to make. She had to decide if she was in or if she was out. She chose out. But by her actions, she taught us kids that doing the right thing wasn't always the easiest thing.

I met my first husband at his house when I was a freshman at Queen of Peace High School. It was love at first sight. I looked at his mother and told her I was going to marry her son. I was fourteen years old. He took me to my senior prom and we were married six months later. I had a choice to make. I had to decide if I was in or if I was out. I chose in.

Over the next sixteen years, we had three daughters and moved five times. He came home one day and announced that he was promoted to vice president and we were moving again, this time to North Carolina. Well, that was certainly not on my list! I packed up and said goodbye to friends and family, leaving my dream home in Palos Park behind, unaware of the fact my life was about to get interesting. As my luck would have it, he was involved with one of the women in the NC office. I had a choice to make. I had to decide if I was in or if I was out. I chose out. But by my actions, I taught my daughters that we do not tolerate unacceptable behavior. I left the next day for Chicago with what I could carry, my three children. I had no job, no money and no place to live. I was in North Carolina twelve weeks.

Once the girls and I were on our own, it was us against the world. I had three kids under ten and needed a plan, a list. First up, get a job, find a place to live, and buy a car. I rented a little house in Hometown that was smaller than my three car garage in Palos Park. The first time the girls walked into the house they asked "Why are the washer and dryer in the kitchen?" "How come there are no stairs?" "Gasp! There is no Jacuzzi, where will we have our bath?" Their little princess lives were about to crumble. Was I making the right decision? Going from poor to rich was easy; rich to poor was another story. We moved in, slept on the floor because there were no beds and ate sitting on the washer and dryer because there was no kitchen table. It was the smallest place I had ever lived in. To this day, the girls speak very fondly about that little house. They never saw bunk beds squeezed into a room no bigger than a closet; they saw a life without fighting. I made the right choice.

We quickly settled into a routine. Between school, work and children I was scheduled every waking minute of every day. I took a job as a dental assistant. My pay rate was $10.00 an hour and my child care was $7.00 an hour. I begged the judge to just let me stay home and care for my children. He advised me to go home to my husband. If I wanted so badly to be a single mother, this is what single mothers do. Right then and there I had a choice to make. I could go back to North Carolina, (he said he would "give up the girl" if I came home) or I could stay in Chicago and be the best tired, broke, single mother I could be. I had to choose if I was in or if I was out. I chose in. I decided right there that I would no longer let a man disrespect me.

I was starting the "Poor Deb" pity party period of my life. I was better than the life that was thrown on me. I was stuck at this ten buck an hour job, bored out of my mind, raising these kids alone while my husband ran off with his twenty five year old secretary. That broad was sitting in my big house, driving my car and taking my vacations. I was angry.

Round two: I was single for seven years between marriages. I moved with my children up to Schaumburg to start my new life. There was something strange about my new husband that no one could quite pinpoint. I didn't care, I was now living in a two income household and my life was getting easier. I made a decision about the rest of my life while I was angry about something else. It was a bad choice.

Soon after we moved in together I realized that his state of mind was suffering. It was noticeable at work and he was fired. I wanted to take him to a psychiatrist. His Mom and Dad, both doctors, decided I was hysterical and told me I needed Valium to calm down. Where was this on the list?

And then it happened. While I was out with one daughter, he acted inappropriately with the other. I had to do something and quickly. I was in a pure panic mode, like a mother bear protecting her young. I took him to the hospital; they handcuffed him to a gurney and took him away. In the next seven hours I changed the locks, made a new lease without his name, went to the courthouse and obtained an order of protection, hired a divorce lawyer and filed a petition for Dissolution of Marriage. *Where the hell is my list!?* I had a choice to make. I had to decide if I was in or if I was out. I chose out. By my actions, I taught my daughters that nobody messes with my kids.

That was only the beginning of my ride down. This marriage was a topsy turvy gut-wrenching, no fun rollercoaster on a broken track. How did I allow myself to be legally married to this person? Why didn't I see it coming? I was the head of household supporting him. I was legally responsible for him. After what he did to us, I had to pay his bills! His two week stay in the psychiatric ward as well as all his doctor's appointments and medicine were my responsibility. A few weeks later he was out of jail, out of the psychiatric ward, living in a hotel awaiting pedophile and divorce charges. He disgraced his family and they all blamed me for reporting him. Good wives don't do that.

On September 6, 2002, I was kidnapped. My husband thought that if I just "disappeared" the charges brought against him would simply go away. Two men took me at knife point out of my home. You are supposed to be safe in your home. I was with my attackers for seven hours. For seven hours, I was taunted and teased, as well as physically and mentally assaulted.

Then there was the car ride. Statistics show once you are moved from one location to the second, a homicide usually occurs. I knew where we were going and I knew I wasn't coming back. There was one point where I was restrained in the back seat of the car where I gave up. I wanted the car to crash so I could die naturally. I had taken as much as I could and just needed it to be over. "Just go to sleep" I remember telling myself, I just couldn't listen to it any longer. I shut my eyes tight. I said my prayers. I thanked God for a wonderful life and fantastic children. I asked for forgiveness. Every person that I had ever met came to me to say goodbye. There was the light, I saw myself at the bottom of the stairs and the light was blinding at the top. I knew this was it. I didn't fight, I accepted it. My Grandpa was standing at the top of the stairs. I became very excited and tried to crawl up to him. When I was a child he fixed everything. He will fix this if I could just get to him. He told me no, not today, I had work to do. I was not finished raising my children, and I couldn't come today.

I woke up to a lot of commotion in the car. They were shaking me and slapping my face to "come to." Right then and there I had a decision to make. I had to decide if I was going to live or die. Was I in or was I out. Nothing else in the world mattered that second in my life besides deciding in or out. Very simple, quick, pick one, in or out, yes or no, what's it gunna be, decide now, ***PICK SOMETHING!***

In, I chose in. I chose not to die that day. I knew I could not physically fight them. I needed a plan, a list, and fast! Separate one from the other, get the car keys and steal the car. Within two hours of my deciding to live, I was alone in their car driving to the police station. All it took was a decision, a choice. I let those idiots terrorize me all day but the minute I took control of my life, the minute I made a choice, I was in control. Big lesson learned that day. Be very careful to whom you give control of your life.

The day after the kidnapping I took a trauma test. I tested out in the highest category a human could be traumatized. I didn't leave the house for five months without someone with me. I lost my job, I went through my savings. For the next two years, I went to court three times a month, once for the kidnapping, once for divorce, and once for pedophile. Where do you work anywhere and take three days a month off? I also had extensive counseling. I never wanted to be one of those people that were "never the same since the incident." I worked hard at getting better.

That was eleven years ago. Since then, I have earned a Bachelor Degree at DePaul University and have had speaking engagements with police and woman's groups. (Shout out to Schaumburg Police Department and all who helped me recover, You Rock!)

Every day in the US, more than three women are murdered by their husbands or boyfriends. My hope and goal is to teach every woman the signs of abuse, so they can make the right choice. People do things in life because they choose to; they don't do things because they choose not to. It is really that simple. Life is full of choices, and those choices shape our lives.

"I am not what happened to me, I am what I choose to become."—C.G. Jung

Deborah McPhee

Deborah McPhee is an Independent Beauty Consultant with Mary Kay Cosmetics, specializing in grooming corporate women for over 17 years. She recently received her BA in Business from DePaul University in Chicago. She can usually be found attending teddy bear tea parties with her two granddaughters. In her spare time, she volunteers with victims of domestic violence. "I want every woman to know the warning signs. Even in a happy relationship, you should always have an exit plan. Hopefully, you will never need it."

Deborah McPhee

Mary Kay Cosmetics

312-533-1994

Deborahmcphee@gmail.com

www.marykay.com/dmcphee

Anna Weselak

"Saying Yes One More Time"

Life for me was the typical image of a suburban wife and mother. I was a former public school teacher who was taking an extended maternity leave to raise my children. Soon after we were married we settled into a suburban Chicago community and decided that we would make this town our home. If we planned to live here and raise a family here, I was set to make this the best community that it could be for our children. I immediately joined the newcomers club, then a woman's club and several other community organizations that satisfied my thirst for leadership and served the community. It was a welcome relief from being a full time mother of twin sons.

Little did I know that just as my sons were facing a new phase in their lives when they headed out the door for their first day of kindergarten, so was I. Since their little sister about to born any day, I was still dedicated to being a full time mother, but with just one baby to care for it was a breeze, and I found myself even more fully involved in my community.

A new organization that I joined was the local PTA at the school where my children were now attending. It was not really new to me since my parents were active members and I was a member at the school where I taught. I did not realize that my reputation preceded me, but some of my neighborhood friends who were also volunteers in some of the organizations that I belonged to, were already members of the PTA. Before I knew it, I agreed to be on the PTA board and within a couple years I was the president of the PTA.

I attended my first PTA state convention while I was a local PTA member and I began to accept PTA positions beyond the local level. I became active on the council and eventually was the council president. That position landed me on a district board of the state where I eventually agreed to become a district director. I now found myself on the state board as a district director who oversaw a whole county in our state with over 100 PTAs. Being intrigued by the National PTA, I ventured out and attended my first national convention in Atlanta, GA. I was hooked and impressed by all the people who held a passion for the mission of the PTA. I continued to accept positions at the state level until I eventually became the State President of the Illinois PTA

In the meantime, my daughter started first grade. I received a call from a local child care center wanting to know if I would like to teach kindergarten in their center. As a former elementary education teacher with a Master's Degree in Early Childhood Education, it was the perfect job for me. It was only a half day position that I could fit around my children's school day. I was delighted to be back in the classroom as well as a mom and a wife and community volunteer. The early childhood center was lenient about my days off so I could attend state board meetings which were held, at that time, during the week. Most of the state board members were not employed outside the home at the time nor did they have young children at home, so it was not a problem for them to meet during the week.

My children were growing up quickly and talk about going to college was in the air. Even with working extra hours, my salary at the early childhood center was not going to get two kids through college at the same time. I therefore started keeping my eyes open for other opportunities.

One of my responsibilities on the Illinois PTA board was serving as the state convention chairman. One of the tasks was to find a printer to print the program book for the convention. The director at the early childhood center recommended the printer that she used. They gave me a quote and their bid was accepted. The convention was a success and the program book looked great. Surprisingly, a few days later, I got a phone call from the owner of the printing company asking me if I would like to come to work for them.

Knowing nothing about the printing business, I was curious to know why they would ask me. He said that they were looking for an outside sales person and that he was impressed with my interpersonal skills. Maybe this was the entre that I needed to venture into the business community. So I quit my job at the center and became an outside sales person for a small printing company in a neighboring community. Fortunately, they were also willing to be flexible in allowing me to work around the hours of my children in school and my active volunteer career which now included serving on the Illinois PTA State Board as well as the General Federation of Women's Clubs of Illinois State Board. My paychecks were bigger and we were now on a steady path.

I learned early on that there is no steady course in this journey of life. I lost my father when I was 30, less than a year after we lost our first daughter who was born full term and lived for 29 hours before dying of Hyaline Membrane disease the day before Easter. Now we were faced with news that my father-in-law had Alzheimer's disease. Fortunately, my husband's family lived nearby but since his mother did not drive, assisting them became part of my husband's daily routine. A few years later, we found out that my mother-in-law had Parkinson's disease and my husband devoted many more hours to overseeing home care providers, doctor visits, and assisting with household tasks. We definitely felt the squeeze of the sandwich generation.

As time went on, there were some personal decisions that I needed to make. There were literally not enough hours in the day to serve on two state boards, work almost full time and stay involved with three active children. The first decision was to choose which state board I would continue to serve. I chose to continue serving the PTA with my passion for education and it was relevant for me since my children were still in school. It was not easy to walk away from the woman's clubs at a time when they were losing members and losing clubs. I am happy to say that years later I am still a member of my local woman's club and still believe in all of the causes that they support locally, nationally and internationally.

My next decision was related to my work. I was getting restless with the printing company and was taking on responsibilities that were not entirely sales and not the part of the job that I enjoyed. I was learning a lot about how to run a small business, how to network, how to get and follow-up on leads, and what the business world was like. I often attended networking functions and Chamber luncheons. However, one of those luncheons was different. One July afternoon, I attended a program on how to be more effective in sales. Based on my sales position, I thought this would be the perfect program for me to attend. I listened carefully to everything the speaker said and realized that it was the same thing that I heard in a leadership workshop at the National PTA convention just the week before. Ahhhaaaa! This is what I would like to do! I would like to speak on topics to help people be better at what they do! I chatted with the speaker after the program and set a date to meet with her the following week for lunch. She introduced me to the DISC assessments. I was hooked! I loved the tool and I would love facilitating this for people in the workplace. Two months later, in October 1994, I launched Weselak & Associates. Nineteen years later I still love what I do!

In the meantime, my volunteer career continued to grow. Now I had a more flexible schedule and time that I needed for board meetings and other events I was able to work into my schedule. At the time when I was elected to the position of Illinois PTA president, I automatically became a member of the National PTA Board of Directors. I continued to serve on the national board in a variety of positions and through a massive board restructuring until it appeared that it was time for me to consider serving as national president.

Much to my dismay, when I was poised and ready to consider running for President-Elect, the nominating committee did not slate me for the position. A young Hispanic gentleman who was new to the Board of Directors agreed to run and to take the National PTA in a new direction. After many long conversations with several members of the current board, I agreed to be nominated from the floor and run for the position of President-Elect. I ran a campaign and was elected as President-Elect of the National PTA in 2003.

One more time, I was reminded that there is a bigger plan in life than I knew and one month after being elected I noticed a lump on the left side of my neck. I went to my doctor to get a prescription for what I thought was a cold that settled in one of my glands. He sent me to a specialist at Loyola Medical Center who took a biopsy that was inconclusive. The good news was that it was not a parotid tumor, but they did not know what it was. One of my sons, who is a chiropractor, assisted me to begin a rigorous treatment plan of diet and supplements. Although the lump never went away, it did not get any bigger—until about 8 months later. I was eventually diagnosed with non-Hodgkin's lymphoma. I did not have time for this! I was running a business and was planning to be installed as National President in nine months! What was happening to me? I decided that life must go on and that I needed to do what I needed to do. I was supported by family, friends and prayer throughout my treatment plan and was installed as National PTA President in June of 2005. I continued to travel, kept my business going, helped my husband through trying times with the illnesses and death of his family members, celebrated all 3 of my children graduating from college, and danced at the wedding of my daughter. Two weeks before my term as National PTA president ended, I was blessed with the birth of my first grandchild and took on the new title of "Grandma."

Life has changed greatly for me since I was a young suburban mother, but I have never stopped giving back to my community. I am blessed with a loving husband, successful children and the grandchildren that they are giving me. I appreciate the love and support of my friends and family. My business continues to grow and I love what I do. Additionally, I continue to be an active community volunteer serving on several community boards including the local Boy Scout Council, as president of the Zonta Club of Oak Brook, my church parish council and Lombard Service League Woman's Club. How easy it would have been to say "no" when I was asked to step up and take responsibility for a committee or an organization, but I have learned the benefits of continuing to say "yes" one more time.

Anna Weselak

As an educator and a teacher with a Master's Degree in Education, Anna Weselak brings to the training field her experience in education, business, and non-profits. Through leading an active life in community and volunteer organizations for over thirty years, Anna has strengthened her leadership skills and knows the importance of interpersonal relationships, teamwork and effective communication.

Weselak runs her own consulting business, Weselak & Associates. She holds seminars, classes, and workshops for a variety of businesses, agencies, and organizations. She has been recognized for many of her accomplishments including: Lombard Woman of the Year, listed in six editions of Who's Who, an Illinois School Board Association Those Who Excel Merit Award, and The Business Ledger Annual Achievement Award and their Most Influential Woman in Business Award. She is a past president of the Illinois PTA and past president of the National PTA. She was named an Outstanding Alumni of Northern Illinois University from the College of Education.

As the CEO of Weselak & Associates, Anna heads a national company servicing a diverse client base by customizing seminars, workshops, and classes to meet the individual needs of each client while being focused on each participant in every class and seminar.

Anna Weselak
Weselak & Associates
316 Manor Hill Court
Lombard, IL 60148
630-889-0626
aweselak@weselak.com
www.weselak.com

Dorothy Rosen

What About You?

Not Satisfied with So-So!

How many times have you asked the question, "How are you feeling today?" With someone answering, "Oh, just so-so."

I could never give that "so-so" answer, because "so-so" = "average" or worse "mediocre." Who me? Mediocre? Do I feel "mediocre" or "average?" And where, when and why?

Are there areas in our lives where we are afraid to admit that we're mediocre, average or just "so-so?" And is that bad? How we answer that honestly and introspectively is the key to shedding the mediocrity and moving ahead.

For me the question is, how do I become my best self? When I work toward becoming my best self, I move away from being complacent with my life. For me, the issue with being mediocre at something is limiting if I am complacent about being mediocre. I have to admit, I am mediocre at many things. And as I write these words, strong feelings stir inside me, because I have a driving desire to be great in all things.

For example, I'm a mediocre athlete. I would have hesitated to even call myself an athlete a year ago. I have no special ability to run, bike or play tennis. Even if I put in thousands of hours on the tennis court, I will never be Serena Williams. I do not have the youth, athleticism and muscle structure of Serena...I don't have the special ability to excel at tennis at her level...and, I don't have her drive to be the greatest at tennis. While I may never achieve greatness with my tennis game, I can still improve my game. And the act of deciding to work harder on my game automatically defeats mediocrity.

My tennis game has dramatically improved because I implemented three strategies: 1) I play more—getting my time on the court helps me build muscle memory, 2) I work with a coach—who teaches me how to adjust my stroke, my game and my stance so that I know how to improve and 3) I channel Serena Williams on the court so that my self-talk no longer says, "Dorothy, you aren't going to win this match. Your serve needs work. What was with that shot? Seriously, why didn't you move to get that ball?" You get the picture. When I'm Serena, I stand differently. I show up differently. I think like a winner...not the little girl whose mother said, "You are not good enough to play with me. Go hit balls against the wall." Like many self-limiting beliefs, my mistaken beliefs about my ability to play tennis happened decades ago with a simple remark. As an adult, it took work to identify the source of my lack of confidence and come up with a strategy to achieve my goal of becoming a better tennis player.

So what are you deciding you want to change in your life? What are your dreams? Are they big enough? Are they audacious enough? Do you have written goals? Or are they in your head? What limiting beliefs do you have about your capabilities? What's holding you back from your own greatness? We all have the ability to do things that we can't even conceive of. All you have to do is watch YouTube videos to see inspirational stories of people who have overcome their own physical limitations to go on and become heroes because they had a burning desire to achieve. A burning desire that overcame all obstacles. Have you defeated yourself before you even start?

My biggest fear is not mediocrity. I am okay with being mediocre in certain parts of my life. In truth, my brain cannot wrap itself around being great at all that I do. My biggest fear is complacency. For me, complacency is the opposite of courage. It means that I have given up striving and moving forward becoming more of me. It keeps me from being fully present in my life. I live my life by the saying, "this life that I am living today is not a dress rehearsal. I get to live this life, this time." This helps me remain focused. It keeps me from becoming a slave to my emails, my text messages, computer games (I'm a recovering addict to many of them) and television. Anything that numbs me and engenders a fugue state where I all of a sudden look up and say, "Wait! What happened to the last hour?" are activities I move away from.

Complacency to me is being satisfied with where things are at...and leads to stasis...so if I'm not growing then what? I am declining. Dying. Growth for me is key. That's why I set goals. Being fully engaged in life I can only walk away from my greatness not into it. I believe that we all have tremendous greatness. An ability to change the course of our lives, certainly, as well as the course of others. I have been given an amazing set of tools...I feel that I have an obligation to hone them over time.

Truly, for me, the difference between greatness and mediocrity lies not in the answer I give but in the questions I dare to ask myself. So the question remains, how do I personally overcome mediocrity? First and foremost, I am open to input...exploring how I show up in this world and identifying what I want to leave as a legacy—my vision. I am coachable. And, I use a simple four-step system taught to me by my mentor. Plan > Do > Review > Adjust. Sounds easy, right? Hah! That's what I thought...and, what I have learned along the way is that my journey has been so much richer than I could ever have imagined.

Goal Setting

I now use a simple formula to develop my goals for the year. I address six key areas in my life that I want to improve and come up with two to three goals for each category. The categories that I use are: Health, Financial, Business/Career, Community, Spiritual and Self Development. And, then, I identify the single-most important thing that I want to work on this month and really put my energy behind that. I may have other goals that can work in concert with this single goal that I can fold in. What I have found is that I become overwhelmed when I want to become a brand new person tomorrow with all of these great new habits...and, when I become overwhelmed I find it hard to focus. My energy dissipates. Focusing on one thing makes it a whole lot easier to get to my goal.

I share my goals with my accountability team, mentor, family, and allies. These are key people that I know will help hold me to a higher vision of myself. It is critical that you enlist the support of others and figure out how you are going to celebrate your achievements. Historically, I failed to recognize how far I came and so, didn't get nourishment from my accomplishments. I'm hiking so fast up that mountain that I forget that when I get up to the top I need to savor that view. As well as savor every stop along the way, the streams I have forded, people I have met, and how my body feels in motion.

Planning

So, let's start at the top, Planning for My Success. This starts with visioning—who do I want to become? How do I want to show up in my life? What is my legacy? The visioning then moves into goal setting. Clearly defined goals. For my primary goals, I think about where I want to be at the end of this year...and the end of next year. Where do I want to be in five years? This helps me set long-term goals that fit into my vision. The important thing, though, is thinking about my 90-day goals...which then are broken into monthly goals... and then weekly and daily goals. It sounds like a lot of work, and, initially, it sure felt like it. However, what I learned was that the first time I did this it was all about my own fears of holding myself accountable.

Do

"Commitment is doing the thing you said you'd do, long after the feeling you said it in has passed."

I don't know who first wrote or said these words...but truly this for me has been the hardest of all things. The planning is easy for me. It took me a bit of time to understand how to plan. What I wanted to track. What I wanted to achieve. How I could map it out. That is a skill and a framework that I could develop and lean on. The other two areas of the formula are also easier for me. Reviewing what I've done and Adjusting for it are a finite process. It's in the doing that I have come to understand myself. It's in the doing that I have occasionally felt overwhelmed. It's my limiting beliefs that have had to be addressed. It's shifting my mistaken beliefs and rules about what it means to move from complacency to greatness. It's learning how to trust in myself with kindness and not just a cold, driving force that is designed to prove to others how smart I am. I can only be there for others and accomplish my goals and visions with the help of others.

I have spent hours working on this part of my self-development. Historically, my limiting belief is the thing that kept me from following through on my commitments to others. Yet, being a person of integrity and known for keeping my word is incredibly important to me. So, get on with the Do! As Yoda sagely counsels us, "Do or do not. There is no try."

Review

I'm back to a paper calendar after years of working with an electronic calendar so I can really see my schedule. The last Sunday of every month I have scheduled the time to review my goals. That's imperative for me, because I am a classic winger. I work hard against this tendency to wing things; because if I wing it, I lose clarity. Without a process, I lose the thread and I never reach my goal. Truly, when I wing it, I'm just being mediocre.

When I review, I look at a number of different factors. How did my month go? What goals did I achieve? Where did I fall short? What got in my way? This time of introspection on my goals is a great opportunity to identify my priorities and my obstacles. Did work obligations get in the way of my family commitments and goals? Did I put everything before my family goals? Did everyone come before me? Did I indulge in my soft addictions (TV, rescuing other people, poor food choices, etc.)?

Adjust

Dwight D. Eisenhower declared, *"Plans are nothing, planning is everything."* In other words, it's great to have a plan, but it gets us only so far.

We need to keep planning because life just happens. Things change. Priorities shift.

After reviewing...How did I do this month? Did I meet my goals? Were they too big? Too small? What did I learn from my activities this month? What do I need to do to reach my goals in the future? What kept me from reaching my goals? I begin adjusting my goals for the following month.

This is not a time to beat myself up. Do you have an "itty bitty shitty committee" who tends to sit on one of your shoulders, or whispers into your ear? I do. I've named her Dottie. (I hated it when people tried to call me that as a child and still do as an adult.) When Dottie starts in on me, I politely—well, not so politely, tell her that I'm really not interested in her input. I don't need anyone judging me for my desire, dedication and commitment to moving my life forward. I am here to continuously do my own work. And, part of my work has been to deal with that part of me that wants to keep me safe and small. Isn't it amazing what our mind does? It buys into what other people want for us. If we conform and remain where we are, complacent in our everyday lives and not living the life that we vision for ourselves, well, two things—1) it's comforting to those around us who are not willing to do their work and who question why we are doing this, why we want so much, and why we aren't satisfied where we are, and 2) sometimes we find it harder to create our own extraordinary vision because we don't believe we deserve it.

So, back to adjusting for next month's activities. I found that when I first implemented this process, I tended to have very ambitious short-term goals (goals for the week or for the next month) and, most likely, my long-term goals were much smaller than they could be. It is my every day activity to change one thing in my life that moves me forward. Historically, I thought I had to make big adjustments until I understood that what I was capable of changing on a daily basis...getting up 5 minutes earlier, going to bed 5 minutes earlier, drinking one more glass of water, making one more call than I did the day before, riding 5 more minutes on my bicycle, reading one more page in a book, one bowl of popcorn, etc. is where real change happens. The incrementality of these actions creates the life that I want. So, what small changes can you make so that you become a goal getter and not just a goal setter? It feels SO much better to reach my goals than to feel like I am constantly failing. My vision helps orient me to where I want to go, while my daily goals help me get to the vision. It is easier to do my daily activities when I know where I am going.

I am living in the present and not wishing my days away thinking about the end destination—I have things to learn along this journey, and I want to make sure that I am fully present for my life. And, along the way, I am course correcting all the time.

I am continuing to evolve. I'm continuing to fight mediocrity in my life. I have a vision. I have goals. I have a process for working them. Do you? Are you overcome with anxiousness thinking about this? Or are you excited? Both are areas to look at in your life. My wish for you is that you have a vision for yourself and that you surround yourself with the people that support your journey as you support theirs.

Dorothy's Recommended Reading List

"Goals!," by Brian Tracy

"No Excuses!," by Brian Tracy

"The One Decision," by Dr. Judith Wright

"The Slight Edge," by Jeff Olson

"The Success Principles," by Jack Canfield

"Transformed! The Science of Spectacular Living," by Dr. Judith Wright & Dr. Bob Wright

Dorothy Rosen

Dorothy's passion is helping people, organizations and companies clarify goals and achieve success. As a senior executive in advertising agencies for over 30 years, she became expert in maximizing time, effort and financial investments for individuals, entrepreneurial start-ups and multi-national corporations as they defined personal and corporate goals, pursued growth strategies and charted new opportunities.

She believes that by mentoring individuals and giving back time and expertise to the business community, society as a whole will benefit. To that end, she works with individuals to help identify new opportunities; and helps businesses develop highly profitable customer loyalty strategies. Dorothy's charity, Flashes of Hope, celebrates the lives of children with terminal illnesses and raises money for research that will eradicate childhood cancers. She is driven by her dedication to her family and her personal growth so that she can better serve others.

She lives in Evanston, Illinois with Steve, her husband, and her children Max and Emma.

Dorothy Rosen
Isagenix
2203 Bennett Ave
Evanston, IL 60201
847-917-1075
dwrosen@mac.com
TheLegacyTeam.isagenix.com

Joyce Klaver
Late Bloomer

My paternal grandmother, a squat, undemonstrative woman, was the first person to indicate that I was worthier than I believed. Allowing me to shadow her, she went about her daily business as she conducted an incalculable myriad of chores. By working alongside her, I gained a solid work ethic. Although in my youthful impatience it hadn't seemed like such a gift at the time. The extensive acreage she managed couldn't be construed as a farm, but it certainly was a self-sustaining homestead. There was little or no time to enjoy the fruits of the labour. If you didn't work you didn't eat. But we did find time to slip away.

She was the one who would initiate me with the ritual of bonding over shopping excursions. Due to her limited resources it was by and large rummaging through bins at the local Salvation Army thrift shop. The hunt for rejected or used items to grace my wardrobe excited me to no end. Even if the garments bore more than a little whiff of the last owner.

It was her love of gardening though that educated me in ways that would elude me for some time. The proliferation of colors & heady scents of flowers, herbs, and an orchard flush with fruit could only be brought forth with a keen understanding and stoic patience. I remember her pruning and shaping a rose bush tucked back into the farthest reach of a waning flower bed. Protected by the sun warmed bricks of the house, two apricot blooms lingered well after the first frost. In her limited, inadequate English she made much of the buds. "Nodobny." She repeated several times. This was the Polish word that I understood to mean pretty. Tenderly cupping the delicate, yawning petals

I could see how much they meant to her. She pretended to shiver, brushing aside the gossamer ice crystals sheeting the ground.

The complexity of communicating without ample English wasn't an issue. As with women communication is by and large measured in touch, body language and facial expressions. What we need to impart to one another…our "teachings" goes beyond the actual words. My grandmother's face suffused with joy said it all. I think what she was trying to convey was simple enough. "Look! See this beautiful thing resisting the pre-winter blight. This is *my* late blooming jewel."

All these years later, I can't help but think that that particular label applies to me. I've been pruned and shaped by events and circumstances in my life. I am without a doubt in the autumn interlude. I've come to understand how many women of my generation struggle to find personal affirmation as they shed the responsibilities of jobs they retired from, children grown and marching to their own drumbeat, or husbands who take up golf and purchase impossibly, impractical cars. What to do now is a question that is often asked. Time is available and the willingness to do *something* creates a whispering urge. We want to become more. We want to create a life well lived! We late bloomers have much to offer.

I come from a long line of strong women. Perhaps not in the sense of blazing new trails but rather accepting what life may throw at us. Making the most of it despite unfortunate disappointments and crushing loss. There are circumstances that might have weakened lesser spirits.

I pay homage to those matriarchal role models. Their stories impacted and influenced mine. Each of them in their own way taught me to listen to my inner voice. Of course, I admit that there were times when I stubbornly refused to heed or credit the experiences and learnings I received. I am a late bloomer in more ways than one. By the grace of a benevolent God I listen now. Carefully! I clearly see how my life was shaped by women I know and have known. As I in turn may shape a willful, lost, questioning sister, daughter or friend.

At times my journey was wrought with self-doubt and floundering. Yet I had the ability to pick myself up, dust myself off and get on with it. If I say I "heard" voices urging me on would that seem...strange?

Do any of you feel something or someone outside your field of vision guiding you? I like to think so. I don't mean to downplay the male influences in my life, but when I recollect defining moments I can usually attribute it to the women around me. Past or present. The wisdom I've gained is like pearls strung together. Each pearl on its own is not worth much, but when collectively put together they are invaluable. Like my grandmother's roses, they should be cherished. They've taken hard work and persistence to acquire.

I remember my mother. Our early relationship left me aching for more. More love. More acceptance. More guidance. Now I see with my hard won insight, the struggle to connect with her was invaluable too. That hurtful, sad path the two of us navigated, ultimately transformed as I saw her give to my children what she was incapable of offering me. She was the late blooming mother. There was a time that I would cringe at the mere suggestion that we were alike. I no longer do that. In fact, I take pleasure in acknowledging that yes there is a depth to me that came through her.

It was only after her untimely death at the age of fifty-nine, (an age I'm inching towards) that revealed my love of putting pen to paper was also one of her pursuits. One I honestly had no idea of. Other than the succinct thank-you notes and grocery lists she jotted down, I was unaware of her desire to express herself through writing.

It was during the wrenching task of going through her personal belongings, a terribly intrusive act in itself that I discovered something that she'd kept to herself. Hidden away on a top shelf of her closet, mixed in with scarves and outdated gloves still sweet with the perfume she wore was an envelope. There in her familiar, neat handwriting began a story of a young girl searching for love and acceptance. In my secret heart, I fantasize that she were here to reveal the nuances of the unfinished tale. If indeed it was a tale. Or why it was never finished. I have a profound sadness that I never knew of its existence. But more so of not being aware my mother was capable of such an endeavor. Were those hopes and desires articulated within those creased pages her own? Something tells me that they were. Reading those few pages spurred me on to make changes. I couldn't in good conscience dismiss my dreams or do as mother did by putting something I cherished on a shelf. I wanted to earn my wings and fly. I took a leap of faith and became a certified Life Coach & Hypnotherapist. Once I stepped out of my fear ridden comfort zone, the universe opened up in ways I'm constantly awed by. I now have the opportunity to uplift and perhaps inspire other women. In that uplifting I gain strength and clarity and live a life beyond my initial belief and expectations. I believe Mom and Grandma would be proud as I am proud of those of you who dream to fly too.

Joyce Klaver

Thirty years have passed quickly since establishing a profitable student housing rental company with my wonderful husband and two sons. This expanded into a management company with our oldest son to ultimately take over the reins leaving me time to ponder my place in the scheme of our planet. My desire to help and inspire other women who have also put their personal dreams on the back burner was the leading force changing the direction of my own life. To that end...or beginning, I took a leap of faith and became an accredited life coach, timeline therapist and hypnotherapist in my mid 50's. Now I'm able to do what I've always dreamed of doing! That is encouraging others to overcome their personal obstacles and to find their true value with coaching and women's empowerment seminars.

I'm passionate to feed the often repressed hunger of my "sisters of the heart" struggling to make their own changes however big or small.

Joyce Klaver

83375 Lahinch Crt

Indio, CA 92203

Joyce.Klaver@yahoo.com

www.Clear-Horizons.com

Linda Lucatorto

That Was Then...This is Now

For most of my adult life, control, order and organization were woven into the fabric of daily living. I made solid decisions and experienced good outcomes. Although the idea of divorce buzzed around in my head for a number of years, I could never have imagined what the reality would bring into my life. My marriage had been suffering from a terminal illness and was an irreparable and injured relationship. I also suffered from very low self-esteem. Therefore, I made the painful decision to file for divorce. I didn't "want" to be divorced. It was a matter of making an arduous choice for my self-preservation.

After 21 years of marriage, I found myself in a place I had never been before. I felt lost, abandoned, overwhelmed and I questioned my self-worth. My life had spun out of control and clinical depression, with all its symptoms, crept upon me like a fog rolling in at night. Everyday tasks became more difficult because I couldn't concentrate. I was consumed with reflections about the relationship...the what ifs, whys, maybe this or that will occur to change the situation and so forth. Whether I was paying household bills, driving to work, tending to my children's needs or trying to get some much-needed sleep, I was tormented by these thorny thoughts. My ability to reason was clouded by self-doubt and a mist of deep sadness dampened my spirit. Fear of the unknown crippled me; hence, I had no direction. Day by day, I stumbled as I tried to find my way out of the blur.

At that time, the summer of 1995, I had been working for a social service agency as the Director of Education. In that position, I developed pregnancy prevention/teen sexuality programs for junior high and high school students.

In addition to creating the various programs, I was the guest speaker in many of the Du Page County junior high and high school health classes. I was passionate about my work and the message I was delivering. Having four or five classes in a row was very demanding and exhausting. I had to be "on top of my game" and relate to the teens in a manner that would capture their interest and gain their trust. I had a straightforward, honest, factual approach. A little drama....and sometimes humor, helped to keep this difficult audience captivated.

When the new school year started in September of 1995, I didn't think I would have the energy needed to stand up in front of a class and give my presentation. I had lost about 20 pounds and was feeling very weak. I brought along one of my other educators as a backup in case I couldn't maintain my strength or present coherently. But I soon discovered that by giving 100% of myself to the students at that present time, I forgot about my problems and personal situation. Being consumed by my work was very therapeutic. Although my marriage failed, I realized that I was a competent and respected professional woman.

My Dissolution of Marriage was granted in the fall of 1997. Ironically, at that time one of my colleagues at the social service agency was also experiencing divorce after a long-term marriage. She was the Director of Counseling. Being supportive of one another, we often discussed our challenges and methods of coping with the stress. Having advanced degrees in counseling, education and psychology did not exempt us from the struggles that any woman would experience during the turbulent time of divorce. We discovered that something was missing. Although church-sponsored support groups were available, there didn't seem to be any local resources for *women only* groups. "Where could we find role models...women who successfully transitioned through divorce and had peaceful, joyful lives? Where could we feel totally understood? Where could we find camaraderie and the hope for a positive future? Where could we gather important information while acknowledging the importance of self-care? Let's become those role models! Let's demonstrate that women can rediscover their strengths and create happy and productive lives post-divorce. Yes, let's concentrate on *thriving after divorce as opposed to merely surviving the divorce,"* we both excitedly agreed! Those were the questions and ideas that led to the birth of The Oasis Experience Inc.® and our mission to provide support, encouragement and education for women facing the storm of divorce. The excitement surrounding the creation of something new and vital helped me to redirect my energy into an arena of hope and enthusiasm. This is when I began to let go of the past and to start living in the present, with great expectations for the future.

In January of 1999, the very first Oasis Experience Spa Weekend Retreat was held in Lake Geneva, Wisconsin. The success of that initial program led to the development of seminars and empowerment groups. For a few years, I continued to work at the social service agency while working on developing The Oasis Experience Inc.® As much as I enjoyed my position as Director of Education; I resigned in 2001 to devote all my time and effort to The Oasis Experience Inc.®

What is unique to The Oasis Experience Inc.® programs is that they are conducted in small group settings which provide a comforting, nurturing and safe atmosphere. Taking the initial first step in seeking help can be a very threatening experience for women. When women join a group or come to their first seminar, they do not walk into a large room or sterile auditorium-like setting. Small groups provide the comfort, privacy and support that are so crucial during this time of upheaval and uncertainty.

The two-hour seminars cover crucial legal and financial issues pertinent to the process of divorce. Attorneys and Financial Specialists are guest presenters. The issue of children and divorce is the focus of another seminar and Child Therapists facilitate those presentations. The empowerment groups focus on dealing with change, overcoming obstacles, re-discovering strengths and planning for a positive future. The empowerment group meets one night a week for seven consecutive weeks. The curriculum is self-developed and discussions revolve around a given topic. Thought-provoking exercises foster great discussions. The group offers women safety, empathy, an opportunity for self-discovery and problem solving. Most of all, the group participants develop a sense of trust and camaraderie. As one of the participants wrote on her evaluation form: *"I thought the experience was offered in a very loving, caring, thoughtful way. Thank you so much for this outlet, the camaraderie and sisterhood...finally people listened!"* Yet another shared, *"Exploring, examining, and understanding the process one goes through during divorce was very helpful. It helped me to further understand the feelings and emotions that filled my existence. I feel less alone."*

Working with hundreds of women over the years has truly empowered me, knowing that I have given them hope and belief that they can create wonderful and rewarding lives, post-divorce.

In 2002 the Collaborative Divorce Initiative came to Illinois and I participated in the first course of "Basic Training". Collaborative divorce is an alternative dispute resolution method that involves a team of professionals. The collaborative approach recognizes that divorce is an emotional life experience that requires legal assistance. Clients have a team of professionals to help support them through the difficult transition of divorce. This is accomplished with a non-adversarial attitude and in the spirit of transparency, cooperation and full disclosure. Professional team members are Attorneys, Certified Divorce Financial Analysts (who act as neutrals), Child Specialists and Divorce Coaches. I was very intrigued by this approach and excited about embracing a new opportunity in the newly-created field of "divorce coaching." My path in life was still revealing itself to me.

I enrolled in a coaching program to become certified and received my CPC designation (Certified Professional Coach) from Grow Training Institute in 2004. In the summer of 2005, I completed a Divorce and Family Mediation Training, which qualified me to apply for membership as a Fellow of The Collaborative Law Institute of Illinois. I became a Fellow of the Collaborative

Law Institute of Illinois in the fall of 2005. This opened up a new door for me. In addition to offering The Oasis Experience Inc. ® programs, I began providing Divorce Coaching for men and women, educating them about their options for divorce, helping them to set realistic expectations and mentoring them throughout the process. Divorce Coaching did not exist when I was trying to keep my head above water during my divorce. As many of my friends told me....I truly made lemonade out of lemons!

My professional designations certainly allowed me to do this work, but my RLE designation (what I refer to as Real Life Experience) helps my clients to relate to me, knowing that I understand their plight from an experiential point of view. I have worked with amazing professionals on collaborative teams and it is so rewarding to know that we have helped families avoid the unnecessary trauma of litigation. I love working with exceptional professionals who are equally passionate about their work. It motivates me and inspires me to keep learning.

I also coach men and women who are not in the collaborative process and are experiencing the frustration and confusion of the court system. Quite frequently, clients come to me in the "contemplating stage" to become as knowledgeable and prepared as possible before making the life-altering decision to proceed with divorce. Additionally, I have worked as a co-mediator on a few cases and have assisted clients with their Joint Parenting Agreements.

By immersing myself in this work, I found true healing and fervor to Pay It Forward. I feel honored to assist so many bright, talented, and genuinely good people who are putting their best foot forward, once step at a time, through such a difficult transition. On my personal journey I have gained confidence and discovered my true self...and guess what? I like me! Although my divorce was a very traumatic and sad event in my life, an abundance of good has sprung forth.

In addition to having my lifetime "I've got your back" type of friends, I have met many new friends. I totally enjoy my peace, freedom, autonomy and independence.

I know how difficult it is to accept change and overcome obstacles. But I have learned that change is a necessary component of life. There is order in nature and the universe. Just think...we would not have butterflies if change did not exist. We would have to endure long, cold winters without the hope of spring. Life itself is an on-going adventure and learning experience. According to Willa Cather, "There are some things you can learn best in calm and some in storm." I learned that the changes which I resisted called forth courage that was held captive inside of me. Accepting and planning for the changes awakened and strengthened my self-confidence. I now view change as an exciting opportunity!

Linda Lucatorto

Linda Lucatorto, M.Ed. in Human Services and Counseling and Certified Professional Coach (CPC) is an educator, group facilitator and public speaker. Linda is committed to educating and supporting people through the divorce process. Being prepared, realistic and calm helps reduce some of the anxiety and stress of divorce. Her goal is to save clients time and money and lessen the emotional upheaval. As a Mediator, Linda helps parents create their Joint Parenting Agreement, keeping the best interest of the children as the focus and paving the way to a cooperative and effective co-parenting relationship post-divorce. Linda has been the sole proprietor of The Oasis Experience, Inc.® since 2008. Linda is a member of the Collaborative Law Institute of Illinois and served a three-year term on the Board of Directors for that organization. Linda also is a member of the International Academy of Collaborative Professionals, American Counseling Association, Illinois Counseling Association, American

Association of University Women and the Co-Leader of the West Suburban Chapter of the Engaging Speakers Network.

Linda Lucatorto
The Oasis Experience Inc.®
Two Mid America Plaza, #800
Oakbrook Terrace, IL 60181
630-887-0374
coachserve@aol.com
www.oasisexperience.com

Suzanne Yvette Oliver

Accidental Courage

There I sat in my doctor's office listening to the words "Your biopsy was positive. You have cancer. It is very aggressive, so we need to move quickly." And then there was something about a port. At that point I zoned out. I heard "chemo" and then "radiation" and "mastectomy" and I left her office without shedding a tear. Instead, I felt nothing but a deep hollow sensation in my body. All of my body...

From early childhood, I'd been through many situations that had resulted in people labeling me a survivor, but this one would turn out to be the last straw. If I survived this cancer, I thought, I would find a way to live a better life and not live in my pain.

As a child, I'd survived teasing. I was adopted and I often heard things like "nobody loves you" and "you were given up because nobody wants you." I found out in the fourth grade that I was adopted – no wonder I was the only blonde in the family! I was so beloved by my grandmother, and also by the most wonderful father, that I never felt like an outsider when I was with them; but the fact that I was adopted left me with a sense of abandonment that became a way of life for me. I was constantly trying to figure out: how do I fit in? To make matters worse, my mother was not a caring woman and we were not close; however, I respected her because my father chose her as his wife. They were married almost 60 years when he died in 2008.

I grew up in Thousand Oaks, California when it was still a suburb of Los Angeles and at that time the city was affectionately known as "Thousand Pilots." Aviation was everywhere and my father was an aeronautical engineer, so I was exposed to flying at a young age. I joined the Navy when I was 18 years old. It was the 1970s, we were just finishing the Vietnam era, and not many women were choosing careers in the military. As a result, I was asked many times why I'd joined the Navy – was I looking for a husband or was I gay? It's funny – now that I look back on it, neither of these reasons would have been bad, but I'd joined because the only thing I wanted to do was fly on airplanes.

I was so focused on airplanes that nothing would stop me from becoming an aviation machinist mate (aircraft engine mechanic) even though there were no openings for a female in a school at that time. Once I found out about the potential to fly as inflight crew, I only had one choice. The only way for a female to learn was on-the-job training (OJT).

I had to learn in the shop and the guys were not too happy to have a "girl" in their midst. It was a grueling period in my life, but I left that duty station with both my dignity and my qualifications to fly as flight crew. I was one of the first women to do this with an ADR aviation machinist mate on reciprocating engines qualification and I went on to work on prop and jet engines. I had survived sexual harassment, which was not even a term yet in use in the Navy.

I vividly remember the flights when there was an emergency. Once, for instance, when I was 19, we landed in Cuba with an engine on fire. Another time I had families of active duty sailors flying into Jacksonville, FL with no guarantee that the nose wheel landing gear was firmly down and locked. I had a job and I was so focused on doing it that emotion flew out the window. I was working in my masculine core at 100% during those times and for me there was no other way.

After a short time, I met an amazing man and it was love at first sight. We dated and talked of marriage for four years. The problem was that he was an officer and I was enlisted, which meant I'd have to leave the Navy to be with him. I was willing to do that but, unfortunately, he died in a helicopter accident before that happened. I was 23 years old and heartbroken. I still miss him to this day but I have learned to live with the happy memories and not the pain of his death.

For the next three years I took as many flights as I could to fill my mind with work. I was not looking for love. Time passed and I met a very handsome, funny man who helped me to feel again.

We were stationed in Pennsylvania, flying together in the squadron, when we decided to get married on Valentine's Day, February 1985. The night before the wedding, he physically attacked me and knocked me unconscious. When I came to, he was very sorry and said he didn't know what happened. What did I do? I married him anyway. That was when the nightmare started. He physically and mentally abused me on and off for the next 10 months. I was all alone in my own head and so far from home that I did not know to run – and run fast. He always expressed how sorry he was and for a few days it would be all right and I would stay. After six months of marriage, I found out I was pregnant. I began to plan my escape to protect my child from his wrath. I had to look inside myself and found that the heart of a fighter is in all of us. I became a warrior to find safety.

Life had other plans. The whole nightmare ended on December 30, 1985. I came home from work to find him sleeping in a chair in the living room – or so I thought. After going into the kitchen to start dinner, I realized the TV was playing cartoons, which was strange. I went back into the living room and then I knew. I was five months pregnant and I'd come home to find my husband dead. He had overdosed on sniffing glue.

The next few days were a blur. I had no idea what to think or what to do. The military took care of everything. We arranged the flight to take him home to Florida and had the funeral on the 4th of January, my 28th birthday. With the support of my friends and my parents, I was able to get through the funeral without going into early labor and losing my baby. At that time, I decided not to wallow in self-pity. On the outside I seemed okay, but inside I was a total wreck.

I stayed in the Navy another two years after my daughter Raechel arrived but it was difficult for a single mother, so after 12 years as flight crew on transport aircraft, presidential helicopters, transport airplanes and fleet transport aircraft I decided to leave the military and try to find work as a civilian.

It was incredibly tough. I was surviving on only a small amount from Social Security for my daughter. I felt like a victim and I was a victim because I acted like one. I wore my label proudly, just as a victim would and without questioning the stories I was telling myself. I'd convinced myself that I was not worthy of a relationship because two men I loved had died.

In the civilian world I started to find some light. I found work in sales, which led to great success and a 25-year long career. Internally I was still a victim of the labels that I believed defined me, but on the outside all was well. I realized that I still had the soul of a woman and that strength would support me in growing and learning to love again.

Then the next blow hit. That day in the doctor's office. So here I was, newly diagnosed with cancer and wondering how I would survive another such blow. All the emotions I'd suppressed started coming to the surface. The literal fight of my life was still ahead of me but I was running on fumes. I decided this was the last straw, though.

I decided I was going to take this step by step. I started trying to put one foot in front of the other at all times... just one step at a time. I would take one step into the chemo room, one step into the doctor's office, into the hospital, into the operating room, into the radiation room, and into my own sickness.

The first round of chemo lasted 12 weeks, followed by the mastectomy and then more chemo for another 12 weeks. For added protection, I had 26 daily doses of radiation.

We started in May of 2001 and after almost a year of drugs and IVs, the doctors declared victory: "Suzanne, we think we got it all."

"We got it all."

I was back on my own with only the stories going on in my head. I had just lost a breast. My posture was terrible. I was always walking with my shoulder bent forward to protect my body and didn't even realize it. I had gone bald and been thrust into menopause at the age of 42, with all the mood swings and hot flashes that entailed. I felt my life was totally out of control.

Then in 2004 my oncologist called to say there was a new test that might explain why my cancer was so advanced and why it was so aggressive. My cancer might've been genetic, she said, and suggested we run the DNA test. Yes, maybe there was an explanation for the beast's arrival. The results of the test did indeed show that my cancer was genetic and they pointed to my biological father. It turned out that I was the daughter of a Jewish man and his bloodline went back to Eastern Europe, probably somewhere in Russia. What a test that was! Not only did it answer my cancer question but I also found out something about my biological family.

However, now another can of worms was open. I was BRCA positive. You may have heard about Angelina Jolie and Christina Applegate and their reasons to have prophylactic surgery. Well, in October, 2005, I lost my other breast and had a full hysterectomy to prevent both breast and ovarian cancer, as the odds of a recurrence of my breast cancer were 97% and I had an 88% chance of developing ovarian cancer as well.

It was then, at the age of 49, that I realized I had become the ultimate survivor. I'd been labeled all my life—by others and by myself—and yet somehow I'd had the courage to overcome so much. I'd had the courage to follow my dreams and fight sexual harassment and abuse. I'd had the courage to love again after a devastating loss and I had the courage to stand up to spousal abuse and report my husband's behavior to the police. And yes, I'd had the courage to fight cancer. But could I say I was thriving and not just living as a survivor? Not yet. I had to look deeper within myself. After all, that's where all the answers are.

After I attended Tony Robbins's Unleash the Power Within seminar, I really started to look within myself and realized that there were many ways to light myself up. I started to learn about gratitude. I had been so angry for so long that it was eating me up inside and I had to let it go. I found that giving back to others became another way to light my soul. It was definitely time to give back.

I've left a six-figure job to emotionally support women going through cancer and to work with women veterans who've had a long hard fight to obtain their dreams. I attribute my "Heart of a Fighter, Soul of a Woman and Body of a Survivor" philosophy to getting me through all the toughest times and being able to joyfully live my life today. Now, as a certified coach for women going through cancer, as well as a keynote speaker on the topic of "accidental courage," I am able to guide women through the reality of the challenges they are facing and help them overcome the major physical and emotional obstacles in their lives.

If you are going through a challenge or are in the life of someone going through a challenge, find out more about how to get the support that is needed to start living life joyfully again by visiting Suzanne at suzanneyvette.com.

Suzanne Yvette Oliver

Suzanne Yvette is a pioneer who was featured in a 1979 Time Magazine article titled, "Women in Non-Traditional Roles." Suzanne's untraditional story is not only an inspiration, but also a testament to the strength of the human spirit. Joining the Navy at 18 and being the only woman on a flight crew is tough enough, but not compared to what she would have to face. In the Navy, Suzanne met her first love and just three years later lost him in a helicopter crash. She found love and married three years later, only to have her husband die 10 months later. Suzanne was 5 months pregnant at the time. This is when she knew that she would need the "Heart of a Fighter." At the funeral, she decided that she would not wallow in loss and pity since she needed to be there for her daughter. She left the Navy after 12 years to support herself and her daughter. She had tremendous professional success only to be tested again. In 2001, Suzanne was diagnosed with late Stage 3 Breast Cancer. She fought bravely and ended up being not only a survivor, but a thriver with a love for life and a spirit of gratitude. Suzanne attributes her Heart of a Fighter, Soul of a Woman and Body of a Survivor philosophy to getting her through the toughest times and joyfully living her life today. To find out more visit Suzanne at suzanneyvette.com

Suzanne Yvette Oliver
Girl on Fire Worldwide, LLC
14313 Lake Mary Jane Rd
Orlando, FL 32832
530-539-4302
info@suzanneyvette.com
suzanneyvette.com

Christine Merrill

Finding My Calling Through Faith

Discovering who you are and who God has designed you to be is quite a journey. At 55, I'm married and have two children and a stepdaughter. My first marriage was very hard. However, my divorce catapulted me into the discovery of who I really am and what makes me happy. This is my second marriage and my husband Bobby and I have been married now for a little over five years. We met online which made for an interesting start. First of all, my husband is in IT and he's a certified accountant. We're polar opposites to say the least. I decided to give him a shot because he rode a Harley and had a therapy dog so I knew he was not only tender but that there was a rebel side. We dated for 19 months before we got married. He proposed to me in Dubai at the Arabian Sea and it was magical. The night before our wedding, I came across the list of wants in a man that I had asked God for. God gave me everything I had asked for except for two things. I asked for tall, Bobby is only 5'7"and I asked for athletic, Bobby does not like to exercise. God has a sense of humor and when it comes down to it, those things don't really matter anyway. God gave me a wonderful husband who encourages and loves me. What I've discovered through many ups and downs is that I have a passion for helping others. I'm entrepreneurial and working for myself suits me and my personality. I'm free spirited, so being confined does not work. As I've aged, I've become increasingly aware that serving, supporting, teaching and helping others to be their healthiest is how I am wired. This is what really excites me! I have two adult children, a son Michael and a daughter Natalie. Natalie married her college sweetheart and they live in another state. I don't have grand babies yet but I'm hoping that will come soon. Natalie and I are very close. I consider her to be one of my closest friends. I not only love her, I like her! Michael, my oldest, still lives nearby. He's a professional artist and he's extremely talented. He's always been creative and he's on his way to creating a name for himself. We see each other usually monthly and spending time with him is always a highlight for me. My stepdaughter Alison is still in college. She's very independent, bright and the apple of her dad's eye. Being a mom has been my greatest blessing and job and I was privileged to stay at home to raise my children.

My husband and I are also the proud parents of two very hairy four-legged girls. Lily is four and Lucy is ten months. They are both Golden Retrievers. Lily is a certified Therapy Dog and Lucy is in training to someday become one. Our first therapy dog, Meg, died a year ago. She was an amazing, intuitive, calm, therapy dog. I'm still grieving the loss of Meg. We had Lily certified when she was just over one year old so for a time we had two therapy dogs and again soon we will be back to two. The dogs are a great addition to my work and my clients love them! Clients look forward to seeing them as much as me! Working at the hospital with our girls is a great honor. My husband Bobby and I see our volunteer work with them as pure ministry. Our dogs truly make others happy! I don't care how tired we are, seeing the affect that the dogs have on someone who is ill or emotionally hurting causes our hearts to soar! We get as much out of serving with our dogs as the people we serve. I'd love to share a couple of stories that stand out in my mind relating to the work with my dogs. The first relates to the last shift Meg and Bobby worked before she died. They walked into a patient's room only to have the patient recognize Meg immediately. She proceeded to tell Bobby that five years before she was hospitalized with severe depression. Meg came to visit her back then and it changed the trajectory of her life. Meg's love toward her gave her the desire and will to fight. The day after Meg went to live with Jesus a large envelope came in the mail addressed to, "my neighbors and parents of Meg". When I opened the letter, I found not only a hand written letter but a memorial brochure. The letter was from our neighbor who Meg and I had visited in the hospital three years ago. My neighbor wrote, "We had just received less than optimistic news when you and Meg came into my wife's hospital room. Meg jumped up on the bed and lay beside my wife. My wife actually smiled, which I didn't think was possible considering the news we had just received. My wife died two days later but I'll never forget the happiness that Meg gave to her". Talk about God's timing. We were so blessed to receive that letter. If he had written it shortly after his wife had died it would have touched us greatly but to receive it the day after our precious Meg died blessed us more than anything! I also want to share a couple of stories about Lily. Lily was a rambunctious puppy and one day she decided to jump up on the massage table with one of my clients on it. I was horrified, but to this day that client still laughs and talks about that day. Another client came to see me one day and was very distraught. She immediately began to cry so I hugged her. While I was hugging her, Lily started to kiss her leg. So the client sat in the chair and Lily put her head on her lap and then the client continued to sob holding onto Lily who never moved a muscle. It has been so very powerful to watch my girls comfort others and bring them joy!

The path of my life journey is one I never expected to be on but one I am so blessed by. We never really know where God will take us but if we remain open we will go places that are very exciting! Along with all of the continuing education classes I've taken as a Licensed Massage Therapist, I've also taken classes in nutrition. Thus, I became certified in Lifestyle Education which now enables me to be a Health Coach. I am able to help my clients make healthier food and exercise choices. Yet again, there is another tool to add to my toolbox.

Another part of my story needs to go back a few years. I have always been thin and very lean until I entered the pre-menopause time of my journey. For the first time other than pregnancy, weight moved in unpacked and planted roots. The closer I got to 50 years old, the more weight I gained and my menopause symptoms increased. When I turned 50, all hell broke loose! I began a three year journey of trying to get relief. Sleepless nights, mood swings, hot flashes, decreased energy and mental fog were just a few of my glorious symptoms. It was a helpless and horrible time in my life. I began working with a functional medicine chiropractor for three years. During this period, she tried every trick in her bag. Herbs, high end supplements, nothing helped. In desperation, I turned to traditional medicine. I visited three gynecologists, and two of them literally told me "to suck it up I was getting old" and the third doctor put me on bio-identical progesterone. We worked at that for four months with no relief. I was so frustrated and so was my Bobby! I would turn into a different person at the drop of a hat. I could be fine one minute and crying the next for no rational reason. Desperate for support, I discovered that few women actually talk about this. I've learned that women in general juggle so many balls at once that they tend to put their needs to the very last.

Then one day about two and a half years ago, client told me to check out a nutraceutical company that I would love. She sent me to her friend who is a distributor for Orenda. She shared some very interesting facts about the products and how they had impacted her life. She gave me some information and I shared this with my husband. Bobby and I researched the company and its products and we both believed the products were worth a try. One of the things about the Orenda products that really resonated with me is that they dealt with the function of balancing the systems of the body, the body as a "whole". A week and half after trying the products I had amazing results! I was sleeping through the night, my hot flashes and night sweats disappeared, mood swings calmed, body aches went away, and my mental clarity and focus improved. I couldn't believe this! I was elated to say the least. It has now become my greatest passion to share my good fortune with other women going through the same nightmare I went through. These products are too great to be silent about. I have witnessed wonderful results because of these products. Numerous men and women suffering from insomnia their entire lives now sleep soundly and travel without fatigue. Autoimmune disorder sufferers now live fully functional lives without drugs, Crohn's Disease improved, IBS sufferers had their symptoms eradicated, and dogs were no longer having seizures. These products are so safe even animals can take them. The healing list goes on. Even though Orenda will not make any medical claims, I have personally witnessed these results and many more.

Another great benefit of these products is weight loss. No matter how much I exercised, no matter how much I deprived myself, nothing took the weight off. Not until Orenda introduced the Clean Burn and Shape. I'm elated that I have lost an additional 26 pounds following the Clean Burn and Shape program. The supplements detoxify the liver so it is able to function and communicate optimally. I never once felt deprived, I lost more weight than my goal, and I'm at the lowest I've been in over 10 years. At 55 years of age I look and feel amazing! I feel 20 years younger and to be honest most people think I'm at least 10 years younger than I am.

I am privileged to be able to lay hands on someone through massage and help them feel better and figure out the root cause of their pain. I'm humbled to help others become as healthy as possible through making wiser choices. Another potential benefit is a decrease in medical costs because of improved health. These products have made such an impact on people's lives. Each of these modalities enables me to help others achieve their whole healing. It is extremely rewarding to see the positive changes in people's lives and a privilege to walk beside them through their journey.

I've been longing to share my story with a broad range of individuals. This has actually been a long time prayer of mine. You can help others and I believe you can do and be anything you want if you set your mind to it. God is so faithful. He has brought so many wonderful people into my life that have helped me, encouraged and believed in me, even when I haven't believed in myself. God hears our prayers and he does want to give us "the desire of our hearts". I am still a work in progress and I will be until the day he takes me home. In the meantime, I will continue clinging to Him and following the path He has for me.

Christine Merrill

Partnering with clients to help them achieve their health and wellness goals. When someone chooses to commit to be healthy, their lives change! Whether it's through massage therapy, diet, exercise, supplements or all of the above it's a thrill to help figure the best course for their needs. Christine Merrill graduated from Massage Therapy School in 2002 with honors. Since graduating, she has completed over 120 hours of continuing education credits. She has added a certification in Lifestyle Education, so that health coaching can be incorporated into her business, Christine Merrill Health. She taught Massage Therapy for 2 and a half years to over 80 students. She is a member of ABMP, is nationally certified with NCBTMB, and is licensed in the State of Illinois. Christine is also certified as a therapy dog handler, volunteering at local hospitals in the Chicago area. Christine, a mother, raised two children. She has led woman's Bible Studies over the years.

She loves to exercise and lives a healthy lifestyle. Being with her family is one of her greatest joys. She enjoys riding on the back of her husband's Harley. Spending time outdoors, working in the garden, taking a walk with her dogs, being near water, dancing, sharing laughter and soul conversations with friends, reading a good book, listening to great music, spending time with God, learning something new, cooking a meal for others and serving others are all things that excite her.

Christine Merrill
Christine Merrill Health
PO Box 340748
Austin, TX 78734-0013
630-750-6238
Christine@merrillhealth.com
merrillhealth.com

Gail Brown

Believe in Miracles

"Be strong and of good courage, do not fear nor be afraid of them; for the Lord your God, He is the One who goes with you. He will not leave you nor forsake you"—Deuteronomy 31: 6

2003 – 2010. Seven years that challenged my limits and my faith. I am a person that values relationships with my family, my friends and my Lord more than anything. My foundation was crumbling.

On Christmas Eve, 2003, my best friend, Laura died delivering her seventh child at the age of 37. Laura was an accomplished nurse and a natural health educator. Her delivery came very unexpectedly and quickly. Before the midwife was able get to her home, she began to hemorrhage. With her six children right outside the bedroom door, she talked her husband through delivering the baby and then bled out in her husband's arms before the ambulance arrived. The paramedics revived her and rushed her to the hospital. I was wrapping Christmas presents, when a friend called me to tell me that Laura was on her way to the hospital and in critical condition. Laura was three hours away in central Illinois. So I fell to my knees in prayer and I begged the Lord to save her. An hour and half later, my friend called and told me that she was gone. I let out a scream of agony that came from the depths of my soul. How could this vibrant, joyful, healthy person be gone? My grief was profound.

In 2004, we moved and our son, Nathan, who I had homeschooled since age five, started high school. It was quite a transition for me. My buddy, with whom I had spent pretty much all day, every day, since his birth, was gone for eight hours a day and sometimes more with football and orchestra practices. I felt lonely and a little lost. That was also the year that my Dad, the most brilliant man I knew, was diagnosed with Alzheimer's disease and emphysema.

In 2005, I suffered a severe asthma attack that nearly took my life. Our dear friend, Mary, who was like another grandmother to Nathan, passed away, and my youngest sister, Terese, was diagnosed with rheumatoid arthritis.

On December 23rd, 2007, my mother-in-law, Marilyn, lost her battle with lung cancer.

In January 2008, my sister, Colleen had brain surgery on a tumor that was diagnosed only months before. Two weeks later, my Dad took his final breath.

In 2009, my husband, who worked in the construction industry, lost his job. I lost my friend, Jane, after a six year battle with breast cancer, and one of my other dear friends, Chris, was diagnosed with lung cancer.

In late spring of 2010, I experienced heart palpitations that woke me up from my sleep. I asked my husband to take me to the immediate care facility to get it checked out. They ran a few tests and were not able to pinpoint the reason why my heart was pounding. They dismissed it as stress-related and sent me home.

In late July, 2010, my Mom was diagnosed with colon cancer and had surgery in early August.

"He giveth more grace when burdens grow greater. He sendeth more strength when the labors increase; to added affliction, He addeth His mercy, to multiplied trials, His multiplied peace." —Annie J. Flint

I think you get the picture. Through all of these events, though, I knew I was not alone. God was right there with me. My friend, Jane, when she was first diagnosed with cancer, had said that she believed that I was a healer and that she knew God heard my prayers, so she came to me for prayer. I assured her that I would pray for her daily, and I assured her that God would gladly hear her prayers, just as He did mine. And here it was, Jane had passed away, my Mom had just had colon cancer surgery and I was not feeling well at all. I was beginning to question whether God still did miracles.

Each day, I write in my prayer journal. On August 21, 2010, I wrote the following:

Lord God,

You are gracious and loving. You do heal the sick and raise the dead. Lord, I pray that my faith can be renewed in Your healing power. I have prayed for many loved ones who have not been healed. Increase my faith. In Your infinite wisdom, You choose who will be healed. You healed Kristin of skin cancer, but you didn't heal Jane. I want to trust you with Mom's life, Chris' life and mine. Please heal us and we will give You all the glory. In the end, You know what's best. I will trust you.

I Love You

I wasn't feeling well at all during the course of that weekend. I woke up on Monday morning, August 23rd, and sat up on the edge of the bed. I felt as though someone had hit me in the chest with a sledgehammer. I was home alone, so I called my sister, Colleen. Colleen called my son, Nathan, who was at work nearby. She jumped in the car and met him at our home to unlock the door. Colleen took one look at me and had my son call 911.

Thankfully, the fire department is right at the corner of our subdivision, so they arrived very quickly. My blood pressure was 60/40 – so low that the EMT said I shouldn't even be conscious. They whisked me the ten minute drive by ambulance to the new Sherman Hospital, which had recently opened its doors, as my husband and my family rushed to the hospital. If the new hospital was not at that location, they would have had to drive me 30 minutes to the nearest hospital, and I would not have survived the trip.

On my arrival, I was in and out of consciousness. They sent me for a CT scan. Thankfully, the CT technician, who performed the scan, noticed something that she had seen on a man just two weeks earlier—an aneurysm which had ruptured in my ascending aorta. She immediately alerted the cardiac surgical team. Amazingly, one of the foremost heart surgeons, Dr. Joong Choh, who specialized in this procedure and travels around the world teaching other surgeons how to do this surgery, was on duty. After quickly explaining the procedure to my family, he rushed me into open-heart surgery. What normally took 4 hours of surgery took nearly 6 hours. Dr. Choh not only patched the hole in my aorta, but he also repaired my aortic valve as well, which also had been damaged.

For an aortic rupture, in which all three layers of the aorta are disrupted, the mortality rate is up to 80%. Fifty percent of these patients die before reaching a hospital. Actors John Ritter and Lucille Ball died from aortic aneurysms. The interesting thing was that I had no blockages, no plaque in my arteries, no high cholesterol, none of the normal things that contribute to heart disease. As I learned from Dr. Choh, aortic aneurysms have a hereditary factor - they run in the family. And stress plays a huge role in it.

I realized that, if any one of the circumstances of that day had not been planned in detail by the hand of the Almighty, I would not have had the opportunity to share my miraculous story with you. I am so grateful for a loving and supportive family and friends who were with me through all of it.

"Miracles never cease to amaze me. I expect them, but their consistent arrival is always delightful to experience." —Mark Victor Hansen

So how has this event changed me and the way I view the world around me? I am confident that "nothing is impossible with God". I realized that God gave me another chance to make a difference in this world. I have decided to look at life differently. When a challenge, a conflict or a disagreement presents itself, I ask God to give me the courage, the wisdom and the strength to surrender it to Him. "Cast all your anxiety on Him, for He cares for you" (1Peter 5:7). I often use a phrase that helps me to put everything in perspective —"In the whole scope of eternity, just how important is this?" That question usually brings me quickly back to a sound reality.

I have also made a choice to see the miracles all around me. I have seen the joy-filled smile of my beautiful granddaughter, Lyla. I have experienced anew the loving servant's heart of my dear husband, Tim. I have seen the love in my son, Nathan's eyes as he gazes into his lady love's eyes. I have seen the Lord heal my mom and my sister. I've seen beautiful new great-nieces, nephews and cousins born to our family. I've spent countless hours of laughter with family and friends.

I have seen miracles daily in my business world as well. Through my wellness coaching with Shaklee, I have seen family and friends with major health challenges turn their lives around with self-care, diet, exercise and supplementation. Some of them have gotten off of dozens of medications and are thriving.

I have come to believe that God gives everyone a message to carry out to the world. Through Engaging Speakers, a networking organization for speakers that I co-founded, we have had the privilege of helping people define their message, refine it and then find the audience that is best served by that message.

Miracles abound in this safe and supportive environment. Many of the people who join Engaging Speakers have amazing stories, personally and professionally:

– Like the woman who struggled to share her passion in a 60-second infomercial, who six months later received a standing ovation from an audience of her peers.

– Or the professional sales trainer and family man, who was inspired (literally aroused from his sleep to do something by divine influence) to write a curriculum to help kids believe in themselves and create a foundation that makes this information available to any school in North America at no cost to the school.

– Or a dad who, upon discovering that all three of his sons and himself were on the autism spectrum, set about on a mission to learn and develop the tools that his boys needed to not just survive, but to thrive in the world around them. Now he's traveling the world teaching and encouraging children, parents and educators with what he's learned.

– Or a devoted mom, who tragically lost a son, who now helps others learn how to grieve and move forward, just as she has.

– Or the retired Army Colonel with an incredible life story about leadership who wanted to become a national speaker and an author, who in just a few short years, is traveling nationally to speak to prestigious audiences. She was invited to deliver a TED talk and just signed a contract with McGraw-Hill to publish her book.

– Or the accomplished speaker, author and coach, who relocated from California to Chicago and was looking to find friends, who is now coaching and mentoring a bevy of new friends on how to speak their way to more business.

I can literally tell you a hundred stories of our members, who are some of the most courageous and gifted people I know. I am inspired and blessed by them daily…all miracles in their own right.

"There are no miracles for those that have no faith in them." —French Proverb

So now, I choose to look for the miracles in every moment of every day that God gives me. How about you? Are you focused on the troubles and the tragedies of your life?

"As a man thinks in his heart, so is he." —Proverbs 23:7

God is still in the business of doing miracles. Join me in choosing to look for Gods' miracles. And to God be the glory for the things He has done!

"For I know the plans I have for you, declares the Lord, plans to prosper you and not to harm you, plans to give you a hope and a future," —Jeremiah 29:11

Gail Brown

Gail Brown is a speaker, wellness coach, mentor and the President and Co-Founder of Engaging Speakers, a powerful networking organization that connects speakers with other speakers as well as meeting planners and resources to help their members speak their way to more business.

Gail Brown's background of over 20 years in field training for the restaurant/hotel industry, as well as two of the top network marketing companies in the industry, has given her the experience and the know-how to communicate a message that gets results. As Co-Founder of Engaging Speakers, Gail is passionate about sharing how any professional can build a speaking business that will go far to differentiate them as the expert in their field.

One of Gail's mentors was Mary Kay Ash, the founder of Mary Kay Cosmetics. One day, while visiting Mary Kay at her home in Dallas, she shared her core beliefs with Gail, "Always put God first, your family second and your career third and you will be a success in business and in life." Gail's greatest joys in life are her relationships with Jesus Christ, her marriage to her husband of 26 years, Tim, being a mother to her son, Nathan and a grandmother to her beautiful granddaughter, Lyla. She has been blessed with a life full of a loving family and supportive friends.

Gail Brown
President/ Co-Founder
Engaging Speakers
627 Grace Drive
Lake in the Hills, IL 60156
888-41SPEAK
gail@engagingspeakers.com
www.engagingspeakers.com

Shaklee Sales Leader since 1997
630-689-7405
BreathingEZ1@gmail.com
http://BreathingEZ.myshaklee.com

Marlene Baczek

Passion to Heal

When I was 8 years old, one of my uncles asked me what I wanted to be when I grew up.

I said, "Happy." He said, "You mean like the dwarf, Happy?" I said, "No, silly, like…you know…happy emotionally." "Good luck!" he said sarcastically. I was somewhat discouraged and knew I had my work cut out for me. I was in search of happiness and it would be a challenge!

I am often asked how I got interested in my profession. So here it goes! After working in a corporate office and sitting behind a computer for almost twenty-five years, I was experiencing pain, recurring headaches and stiffness all over my body. I thought *that this cannot be good.* Even though I was active and exercising, I was experiencing physical pain that was leading to irritability, fatigue and emotional turmoil.

I didn't want to accept that taking a pill was going to make me feel better. It might do so temporarily, but not in the long run. My instincts told me that there had to be another way. What was going to help my body heal itself?

I decided to try a natural approach to my healing journey. In 1999, I received an ancient Tibetan healing art, a hands-on healing called reiki. I had long-lasting positive results. I thought that *I can do that!* I decided to become a reiki practitioner.

A friend suggested that I see a chiropractor. Wow! I never thought of anything like that. So I did. After some time, I started seeing an acupuncturist trained in Traditional Chinese Medicine. I then began to receive therapeutic massage on a regular basis. The results of these treatments were extremely beneficial. It was like something was guiding me to obtain a body, mind and spirit free from turmoil and to create peace, tranquility and happiness. I had enough of the opposite.

I made a decision to try something new. I thought to myself, *I can do this! I can help other people with their health as I did mine.* I had to make some changes, which included both lifestyle changes and going back to school. Education!? At my age…could I do this? That's right, Marlene…just talk yourself out of it! Then I prayed about it and God said, "Go for it! I'll take care of you." Thank God I listened to God!

It's really nothing less than a miracle. It's not like I woke up one day and said, Gee, I want to practice Chinese Medicine. Actually, it did kind of happen that way. It was waking up to awareness. Sometimes you can plan all you want and things may never come to fruition. Then bam!! Suddenly a spark ignites and you admit that you need help and surrender. Then the gift appears right in front of you. When you let go, you are ready to receive new blessings.

Let God carry your baggage

There was a lot of prayer and meditation. I had to learn how to listen. I couldn't ask without an open heart that was forgiving and empty of resentment and anger.

Old Chinese Proverb: "You can't fill a full vase"

I remembered that in college a sorority sister wrote in my pledge book, "Success comes in CANS not Cant's." So I said, *I CAN do this… I can become a natural health practitioner.* I am now an acupuncturist (trained in Traditional Chinese Medicine); massage therapist and reiki master teacher.

Do you believe in "divine intervention?" Well, I do because I've experienced it several times. That's exactly what it felt like when I made the decision to change my career. Like a light bulb going on. Somebody threw a switch. It felt like time stopped. It was a tingling, shiver going through my body like electricity. Like an electrical charge!

The change itself was over a period of time. However, the thought of making a decision was brewing for a while. I just had to be open, aware and willing. I didn't know at the time that this would be my new profession. I was just going to do it part time. But it was like something was guiding me and protecting me.

Yes! I made a decision. It was like jumping off the diving board at the pool. I was moving up to the next platform and the next level. Trying new things was very exciting and I liked the feeling. I could tell that something was brewing in me and that I was fulfilling a desire and a passion. It was a feeling of joy mixed with fear of the unknown like I never experienced before. I prayed! I moved forward and accepted the feeling of being guided to do something more. Yep! That's right—guided. Like something was building a path for me and all I had to do was to listen and act.

That's when I experienced it. Happiness…instantaneously!!! Like combustion. In Chinese Medicine, it is the element of fire and emotion. Joy. Like a jolt of electricity or a bolt of lightning.

I got hit by lightning

I realize that many of us will never experience the feeling of being hit by lightning. Well, I did, and I live to share the experience. It's a feeling similar to "waking up to awareness." I've included my story in my book *Don't Let Your Qi Loaf.* The word *qi* in Chinese means *energy.* That's why I'm called "Qi Queen Marlene." Now you know my secret! My friend Harvey ("Cookie Man") gave me the name "Marlene the Massage Machine." After finding my passion for healing through accessing qi or energy, I decided to move up to the next platform.

The lessons I learned in my search for happiness and finding my passion

Happiness

Yes, it's true that happiness is very similar to getting hit by lightning (only not getting injured or killed). It is fire, warmth, combustion and instantaneous. It doesn't last. It happens quickly and then it leaves us. I experience this when I conduct "Laughter Yoga" workshops. When you laugh for no reason, the joy you feel instantly is amazing. Starting with a smile, then giggling, then contagiously sharing the gift of laughter. It has to be the easiest way to experience instant gratification and happiness. Then it's gone. We can recreate it for ourselves at any moment at any time. As we string the moments together, we then may have a chance of it lasting.

Maintaining this feeling is the challenge. It does not mean to laugh all the time. That would deplete your internal energy or yin as well as your essence or *kidney qi*. In Traditional Chinese Medicine, this is connected to the inseparable relationship between fire and water and the interdependency of *yin* and *yang* (the g is silent): a never ending and continuous flow of energy.

Heart qi: the element of fire, the emotion of joy
Kidney qi: the element of water, the emotion of fear

Laughter and love

I used to say that love is the universal language. Now that I have experienced more laughter in my life, I realize that laugher creates a language of its own. Laughter creates joy and when we are joyful we can all experience love. If you would like to learn more about my Laughter Yoga workshops go to www.lafandluv.com.

Work is a 4 letter word that ends in K

Do you believe that work is work and play is play and never the two shall meet? Work and play do not have to be separate. Happiness and passion associated with your job or occupation *should not* be a new concept for those who want to experience true happiness.

The possibility to be happy and passionate about your job is not a long shot. Passion will happen naturally if you find something that really makes you happy. If you don't receive satisfaction, then it's a chore or a task.

Can it really be possible to co-exist and to co-mingle your source of income with true happiness and passion? *Well, if you don't go for it, you'll never know!*

How to Measure Your "Passion"

Passion Criteria	Mind Body Response
1. Does this bring me happiness or not?	Do you feel a spark? Where in your body?
2. Have I received satisfaction?	Do you feel calm and peaceful?
3. Would I do it again?	Do you feel excited?
4. Can I laugh at myself?	Do you feel nonjudgmental?
5. Am I smiling?	Do you feel warm? Where in your body?

Joy or Fear and the Flight or Fight Response

Think of a toddler who wants to be picked up, thrown up into the air and caught by Mommy or Daddy. Once they experience the joy of flying through the air and their mother or father catching them safely, trust and love has been built. A euphoric feeling has been registered in the neurotransmission pathways. "Do it again! Do it again!" they cry out. And that marks the first experience of the flight or fight response.

The flight or fight response or reflex is a human being's reaction to joy or fear. One causes the feel-good chemicals to be released to satisfy us and calm us and the other causes blood to go to the extremities so we have the ability to run away from the saber tooth tiger.

How to Find Your Passion

Stay away from "Qi Suckergist"

Stay away from those who rob you of your energy or *qi*. They will drain you if you allow them to. These vampires deliberately want to harm you. They are selfish, dishonest, needy and distracting. Be aware and develop your ability to eliminate, disarm or neutralize the people, places and things that bring you any suffering.

What's Your Saber Tooth Tiger?

Do you want to experience happiness and joy? Then you need to figure out what constitutes your own saber tooth tiger. The way to obtain happiness, joy and satisfaction can sometimes be found through a process of elimination. That's right! List a few things that you know **do not** bring you joy or happiness. Below are some examples. Start your own list.

1. Bad memories of people or situations
2. A cold bedroom
3. Burnt pizza

Follow your interest

We all have interests or things that we always wanted to pursue.

1. What type of people would you like to surround yourself with?
2. What type of places do you see yourself spending time at?
3. What animals, vegetables or minerals interest you?

What are you good at? What are your talents? The Three A's

We all have a gift or a talent that we enjoy, something that separates us or makes us unique. As much as we may all like a challenge, we all should identify our personal "Gimmick"—a God-given talent.

1. Activities
2. Accomplishments
3. Awards

For me, finding happiness was finding my passion

I've decided to share my story in the hope that it will bring some wisdom to individuals who are still searching for true happiness. Continue to do the things that bring a smile to your face.

By sharing my experience I can receive joy in knowing that a positive, happy person can make a significant change in their world by being contagious to others around them. Like tuning the radio dial to the proper station or creating a vibration like an electrical current.

When you find your passion you will no longer be searching for that burst of energy to create satisfaction. Your passion will be your spark. You will be able to ignite happiness at any moment, at any time, no matter what. It's just like laughter! Try it! It works!

If you would like to learn more about qi and how energy effects your emotional and physical health, please refer to Qi Queen Marlene's book *Don't Let Your Qi Loaf.* This book explains how happiness, longevity and wisdom can be found and lead to a healthier lifestyle.

Marlene Baczek

Marlene Stanley Baczek has a mission to awaken people to their self-healing abilities and to educate them about natural choices which promote better health.

She is a board-certified licensed acupuncturist massage therapist, reiki master teacher and clinical thermographer. She is also trained in advanced bodywork techniques. She offers a motivational workshop called *Don't Let Your Qi Loaf* and has developed a unique form of therapeutic dance called "Anna Marlena's."

Marlene decided to start writing after experiencing a hiking accident which resulted in a multiple fracture and dislocation of her ankle. After surgery, she contracted MRSA (methicillin resistant staphylococcus aureus), which is a type of staphylococcus bacteria (staph) that is resistant to beta-lactam antibiotics. Since this was life threatening, Marlene was hospitalized for 3 days and had to use a wheel chair for 8 weeks. With 9 screws and a plate in her ankle, Marlene had to teach herself how to walk again. This challenging experience enlightened her awareness of how passion can overcome fear and shape our lives.

Marlene Baczek
Healing Your World
847-361-6398
Marlene@healingyourworld.com
www.healingyourworld.com

Alyssa Horton
Taking Control of My Life

At the most pivotal point in my life, I had no idea what I was doing. Financial aid applications were buried under stacks of hospital bills. Every counter and tabletop in my house was littered with calling cards for the optometrist, pulmonologist, pediatric surgeon, and physical therapist. The sink was full of bottles, and the scent of dirty diapers seemed permanently etched into my sinuses. It's hard to believe that one year earlier I was 16 and the future was just a far-off concept.

In high school my time and attention were split between friends, homework, sports, and recovering from an eating disorder. My family supported me as I struggled to conquer depression and self-esteem issues, and by my junior year I was ready to put all of that behind me. I began to treat my body with respect and started talking to college representatives about my future. I toyed with the idea of being a teacher or a nurse, because they both fit my desire help people.

All of my plans came to a screeching halt on November 1st, when I found out I was pregnant just two months into my junior year.

At first, I was in shock. The results of the pregnancy test were very clear, but I couldn't wrap my mind around it. I have wanted to be a mother for as long as I can remember, but my vision of the future had always come equipped with a husband, a master's degree, a stable job, and a house of my own. In a single day, all of my priorities changed. I put off college visits to schedule prenatal care.

I lost a lot of friendships at a time when I needed support the most. I felt like I was functioning on auto-pilot, going to school and trying to block out the rumors and demeaning jokes I heard around every corner. My house had always been a safe, inviting place, but even light conversation was overshadowed by the news that all of our lives had irreversibly changed. I had never experienced such a deep fear of the unknown.

The decision to parent came easily to me, but I knew nothing about parenting besides what I had put my own mother through. The decision to ask for help was much more difficult. My high school social worker referred me to a nonprofit organization that helps pregnant and parenting teens, which was the first time I had heard of Teen Parent Connection. As far as I knew, I had never met a teen parent before; I didn't realize how prevalent teen pregnancy was, in my country or in my community. When I attended my first group meeting, it was like a veil had been lifted. I immediately felt at home with these girls who understood how it feels to be treated like a child and expected to succeed at parenting. I attended groups and poured over books about what to expect in my pregnancy, but nothing could have prepared me for what came next.

My mom was with me at my very first ultrasound, and we were both rendered speechless when the ultrasound technician asked a question that changed my life: "Did you know you're having twins?"

Just when I thought nothing could surprise me anymore, I was proven wrong. This revelation meant that my pregnancy was considered high-risk, and there was a chance I would deliver a few weeks early. But more important, I wasn't just having a baby anymore; I would have an entire family in a few months.

The first step to realizing any of my dreams was finishing high school, which I had never considered an obstacle before. My counselor and I created a plan for me to take on a heavier load of classes and graduate a year early and with this goal in mind I finally felt like I had regained some control over my life.

Once I was halfway through my pregnancy, I had gotten used to dealing with invasive personal questions from teachers, nurses, even the barista at Starbucks. It didn't scare me anymore when strangers at the grocery store touched my belly without asking. But on the day that my mom and I started a baby registry, I went to a routine ultrasound that ended much differently than expected. The technician smiled as she pointed out their heads, legs, and tiny feet, but then she abruptly stopped talking. She excused herself to get the doctor, and my heart sank.

In a few moments that felt like hours, the doctor entered my room with a wheelchair. I couldn't breathe. I could tell something was wrong, but I didn't understand a word she said, it was like she spoke another language. I only remember a blur of colors and sound, my heart pounding in my throat, and suddenly being wheeled through a set of doors that read Labor and Delivery Unit. That jarred me out of my fog, because I knew I couldn't be in labor, I was only 24 weeks pregnant.

My trip to the hospital that day turned into a month and a half of bed rest. I was having contractions just a few minutes apart, and I knew that if my sons were born at 24 weeks they didn't have a good chance of surviving. Making the decision to parent was the most significant thing I had ever done, and now I felt like that choice was being taken out of my hands. I was so attached to my sons already that I couldn't imagine leaving the hospital empty-handed. Most friendships fell apart at this point, but in my loneliness I had more time to focus on finishing my classes from my laptop in my hospital bed, and stay on track with my aggressive plan to finish high school early.

I was on a cocktail of medications to keep my sons from arriving too early, but eventually they stopped working. Around 2:45am on May 2nd, I went into the operating room for an emergency c-section. My mom, who was scarily intuitive at this point, had decided to spend the night in my hospital room and was there to hold my hand through the procedure.

Although I had anticipated a magical moment in which I met my sons for the first time, it broke my heart to see them both wrapped up in tubes and wires. I was in awe of how tiny they were at three and a half pounds each; I felt like I needed permission to hold something so fragile.

Returning home while my sons were still at the hospital in the neonatal intensive care unit (NICU) was devastating. I spent the next month and a half visiting them every day and finishing my schoolwork. I graduated and had already signed up for classes at the community college when my sons were finally ready to come home.

After nearly two months, I left the hospital for the last time, with a baby carrier on each arm. That summer I learned so much about parenting that no book could have prepared me for: the frustration and guilt when my sons wouldn't breastfeed, the sleep deprivation so extreme that I felt intoxicated, the love so deep that I couldn't remember what it was like not to be a mother.

The parenting books also didn't prepare me for the struggles unique to being a teen parent, like realizing that your boyfriend at 16 may not be the person you spend the rest of your life with. Or feeling helpless when your babies are sick, because you already know you're going to fall behind in school, and your employer can find another cashier to replace you in a heartbeat.

My confidence built every week as I attended parenting groups and met with Emily, my home visitor from Teen Parent Connection. Once a week she would spend an hour talking with me about child development, community resources, setting goals for my future, and how I could achieve them. I felt educated about the decisions I was making for my family, and empowered to create the future that I wanted my sons to have.

I was offered a chance to volunteer for Teen Parent Connection by sharing my experience and talking to high school students about preventing teen pregnancy. At first I was hesitant, because I honestly couldn't imagine a world without my sons. But I thought of my younger sister, just entering high school, and how I didn't want to see her forced to make difficult decisions about her future at such a young age.

When I went to a school for the first time and opened up to those students, I realized there was incredible value in sharing what a teen pregnancy really looks like. My message was clear: as much as I love my sons, I would have an easier time providing for them if I had experienced my pregnancy after finishing school. I wasn't prepared for these responsibilities at 16, but I worked hard to prepare myself, and I continue to work hard every day.

My volunteer opportunity led me to earning a position on Teen Parent Connection's staff. Now I share my experience with hundreds of students in schools and community groups, hoping to make an impact on the decisions they make in their own lives.

My life doesn't look much different from the outside, now that my sons are almost four years old. I still live with my parents, I'm still in school, and there still aren't enough hours in the day for all of my priorities.

But I have completely transformed as a person.

The moment I found out I was pregnant, my childhood ended and a new life began. I've heard more than once that experiencing a teen pregnancy means you have to grow up overnight. But I found it wasn't that simple; "growing up" wasn't an accomplishment I could check off a list, it was making a series of decisions every day. Four years later, I still have to decide that I am going to get out of bed, get my sons ready for school, get through my own school and work schedule, and resist the temptation to crawl back under the covers and sleep all day.

Even though I talk to teenagers about how making safe sexual decisions can determine your future, I don't believe that my pregnancy sealed my fate. I believe that the choices I've made every day since have been even more powerful and impactful than any single event in my life.

One of the greatest moments of my life was being called a "success story" by Teen Parent Connection and realizing that I have amounted to more than I originally thought possible. At twenty years old, my journey is far from over. Most of my goals are long-term, and I have to take them on one day at a time. Someday my family will have our own house, a car, and my sons won't have to share a room with their mom.

In the meantime, I am in a relationship with someone who respects me and loves my sons immensely. My little boys, Jackson and Robbie, are lucky enough to live with their grandparents and two aunts who spoil them with love and attention. Right now, the world revolves around them, and that's exactly the way it should be. I'm working towards my bachelor's degree in social work because I know that I can still fulfill my dreams, and that getting my education will improve my sons' lives as well.

But I won't stop there; I want to help empower people who feel powerless just like I did. I have taken control of my life in a way that I didn't know was possible, and now I am unstoppable. At 16, I refused to be a statistic, and now I refuse to settle for being mediocre.

Alyssa Horton

Alyssa Horton is a young mother and full-time student. Growing up in Naperville, IL, she was an athlete from an early age and involved in theater at Naperville Central High School. When she became pregnant at 16, Alyssa received services from Teen Parent Connection, a nonprofit organization in Glen Ellyn, IL. She graduated from high school a year early and began taking college classes while raising her twins.

Alyssa has been called a "success story," and she attributes her success as a parent to her strong family support, as well as the services offered by Teen Parent Connection. These include support groups, home visiting, an incentive-based Parent's Pantry, and a staff that works to be personally involved with each one of their hundreds of participants. She now works for this organization as a Peer Educator, talking to schools and community groups about healthy decision-making and preventing teen pregnancy.

Alyssa is currently finishing her Associate's Degree and has been accepted into the School of Social Work at Aurora University. She will graduate in the spring of 2016, and she plans to devote her life to assisting and empowering those in need.

Alyssa Horton
Teen Parent Connection
475 Taft Ave
Glen Ellyn, IL 60137
630-790-8433
alyssah@teenparentconnection.org
www.teenparentconnection.org

Deborah Todd
On the Other Side of Fear

Living with fear and fear-busting have been patterns for growing up in my family. Due to being born prematurely, my father has had a relentless challenge surrounding reading and writing. Dad has never liked the word "illiterate," so I won't use it here out of respect for him. He has given me permission to write about him, sharing with me that letting the world know really doesn't matter to him at this late season of his life.

Growing up, I didn't realize the challenges my dad was facing day in and day out, until a time when I was renewing my driver's license at the DMV. Dad accompanied me because he also needed to renew his license by taking the written exam.

I can honestly say that I was shocked at the severity of his reading challenges. He couldn't read anything on the exam form. I was confused. I was twenty years old at the time. How could I never have noticed the scope of his reading disability? The way Dad walked through life had always shown me how smart and talented he was. Dad—a fun-loving, personable guy who never let his disability stop him from making a good living and loving people.

Now that I have had an opportunity to observe his maneuvers for masking his reading disability, I realize how he is pushing through fear every single day. There are very few people who know about Dad's reading challenges. He has found a way to face his fears by taking control of what he needs to do in order to avoid that exposure. I can only imagine how stressful it must be to live your life continually at the risk of being exposed. Almost like a criminal, thinking there's always a chance you'll get caught. Actually, my dad uses that exact word choice when I'm helping him with his affairs now: "I don't want to get caught."

One of Dad's leaps of courage came in the '60s, when he took a risk with a friend of his to learn the operating engineer business, developing a skill for moving earth and gravel with heavy equipment. In an effort to feel valuable and to always look as if he were smart and knew what he was doing, he worked harder than his counterparts. For him, self-worth came only through challenging himself to push through fear in order to make a living and provide for his family. When he retired, it took two men to accomplish the same amount of daily work that he had accomplished during those 40-plus years.

Reflecting on my childhood, I have come to recognize that I grew up in a family whose bar was a bit lower than most. I don't mean that in an unloving way—only that daily living *was* the high bar. Fear permeated my childhood. By fifth grade I had become a chubby ten-year-old (I prefer "chubby" to "obese," "overweight" or "fat"). I was afraid of nearly everyone, especially adults, and I was taunted on a regular basis. "Two Ton Toad" was the nickname assigned to me by my classmates as I reluctantly walked through the halls during the remaining years of school. Most of my childhood was spent trying to be invisible so that no one would notice me to tease me.

I'm sure you can imagine how my self-esteem barometer chose my spouse. "Oh, somebody likes me...great, let's get married!" was the seemingly affirming message from my inner voice

Fast-forward nearly two decades. One Sunday morning, I stood up from the breakfast table and simply said, "I'm not doing this anymore." That morning was the most pivotal moment in my life. To this day I don't know where that voice came from, but it uncontrollably burst up through my body and bubbled right past my lips.

My friends and family believed mine was the perfect life. Suffice it to say that our family and friends did not live in our house. I decided in that brief moment that I wasn't going to be emotionally beaten down anymore, especially in the presence of my then nine-year-old daughter.

Leaving was the least of my troubles, although fear hovered like an angry storm cloud because I hadn't really thought my leaving through. I had no self-supporting job and no money of my own. But having lived the first half of my life in the throes of fear, I was ready to do life differently. That pivotal moment was 17 years ago, and I am happy to say that through my own self-reflection and personal growth I have made it to the other side of fear happier and on a path I love.

I have been blessed along my soul-searching journey by many messengers. I was guided and led first by a Louise L. Hay book that was given to me: *You Can Heal Your Life.* The messages in Louise's book caused me to think about the way I was seeing myself, others and the world around me. I examined where my beliefs were coming from, and realized that some of my self-limiting beliefs weren't even mine. I was living my current life immersed in fear the same way I had lived my childhood. Could I be, in part, responsible for how my life was playing out? This was my first message —a catalyst for valuing myself more and realizing that if I could change my thinking, I just might be able to change my life.

The next messenger was a woman who gracefully walked into my life for a moment and then blew out like a warm breeze. We had taken the same personal development workshop and partnered up for one of the exercises—no accident, I'm sure. There was something different about her that piqued my curiosity. In our interaction, she revealed to me that she was a life coach. Since I was unsure what a life coach was at the time, she explained that life coaches help people to live a more fulfilled life. I was intrigued; you see, I had been unofficially helping women get on the other side of their mediocre lives by pushing through fear and loving themselves more fully. I asked myself, "What if I could actually make a living helping people live the lives they imagine?" I was so excited contemplating the possibility that as a skilled coach I might help women walk in courage to change something about their lives.

It wasn't an easy decision to attend coaching school. Working a full-time job to get my daughter through school was the focus of my life at the time. I remember a phone conversation with the admissions coordinator at the coaching school. I panicked: "This is a lot of money for me, and what if I don't end up liking the classes for coaching?" She said, "Tell you what: If you go through the entire first weekend and, after Sunday's class, you decide this isn't for you, then call me on Monday morning and I'll give you a full refund." I was thinking to myself, "Phew, thanks, I can breathe now and let go of the 'what if' worry." Well, no need for a refund: I was addicted after an hour of class. Okay, maybe "addicted" isn't a word a coach should use. How about "engrossed" or "captivated"? I knew this was where I was supposed to be. Thank you very much, admissions coordinator. Sometimes all it takes is someone to recognize your fear and throw you a sort of life preserver so you can get on the other side of that fear. Hmm…feels a bit like coaching!

One of my favorite quotes is from Brendan Francis:

"Many of our fears are tissue paper thin, and a single courageous step would carry us clear through them."

I sense that most of us feel that our particular fears are much stronger than tissue paper. It can feel that way if we aren't used to stepping through the fear. For example, a common fear shared by many people is that of public speaking. Jerry Seinfeld comically said, "People would rather be in the casket than give the eulogy." Talk to a Toastmaster (a speaking organization) member. Many a new member began terrified to speak in public. It's been my privilege to witness many members stepping courageously into public speaking to get on the other side of that fear. Now many of those fear-busting speakers are well known and have accomplished great things, impacting countless lives with their messages.

I am one of those people. With a history like mine, you can imagine how afraid I was to stand up in front of a group of people and deliver a speech. Speaking meant I couldn't be invisible anymore—terrifying for me on so many levels.

Although staying in one's comfort zone feels like a cozy comforter, the rewards of stepping through to the other side can feel a bit exciting, more like a silk sheet. Think of a time when you were afraid of doing or being something. What motivated you to step through? If there's something that you're afraid of now, imagine the possibilities that await you on the other side of that fear. Does the other side of fear inspire you; do you have a strong answer to your "why" in terms of getting there? Look at what's possible by stepping through, and try not to get hung up on the "how" of your possibility. Standing in the "how" has a way of sabotaging our start before we've even begun. Perhaps it's about the decision: did you decide this is what you want, or are you just playing around with the idea of what you want?

I'm not saying it's always easy to decide; even my dad had to make a decision not to allow his challenges to impact his ability to provide for and take care of his family. I think he'd say that the decision to take a risk with the operating engineer career was one of the best decisions he ever made in his life. It took me a long while to leave my toxic environment. When it was time for coaching school, I was afraid of wasting money by registering in the event it wasn't the right idea for me.

If I had to take that last sentence one sentence further, I'd call myself out here: my inner critic's voice was telling me a story, a story filled with doubt around being a great coach. Had I not pushed through to get on the other side of fear, I most likely would not have been able to write this chapter, either.

What are your dreams or aspirations?

Write them down, right now!

_____

_____

Keep them in an area where you can read them often; if you're a visual person, construct a vision board around your vision.

Create affirmations around your dreams. Make sure they are positive, personal and in the present tense.

_____

_____

Remember, you are more than your saboteur or inner critic thinks you are. Surround yourself with people who will pump you up, not pull you down. Remember that every time you get on the other side of fear you expand your comfort zone, which in turn helps you step more fully into the GREATNESS of the wonderful you that is already there.

If you want something you've never had, you've got to be different or do something you've never done. That means go for it without limitation. There is no failing, just not getting the result you intended, which allows for grace.

Go forth in GREATNESS and embrace with courage whatever is calling you.

Deborah Todd

Deborah Todd, CPCC, PCC, is a highly interactive certified professional coach who has the ability to help people push away the mind and fear barriers that are stopping them from living their best lives and careers. Coaching with Deborah offers clients new insights and perspectives along with the choice and accountability to live an empowered life. Deborah works with clients looking for work-life balance, and with those in career or life transitions. She practices and utilizes many alternative methods, such as guided visualization and Reiki, to expand the client experience.

Along with Deborah's professional certifications with the *Coaches Training Institute* and the *International Coach Federation,* Deborah is the first licensed Louise Hay-certified *Heal Your Life®* teacher in Illinois, teaching empowerment strategies for positivity and possibility thinking. As a Toastmaster and motivational speaker, Deborah also presents several empowering workshops and has been described as energetic and passionate about helping people live a life of choice and fulfillment. In her playtime, Deborah can be found performing as one of sixty voices in the Glen Ellyn–Wheaton Chorale. Deborah enjoys gardening, music and spending time with her family, especially with her one-year-old twin granddaughters.

Deborah Todd
Deborah Todd, CPCC, PCC
Geneva, IL
630-915-7309
deborah@lifecoach-deborah.com
www.lifecoach-deborah.com
www.thoughtshakers.com

Tina Dunn

Somewhere Over the Rainbow

"We want you to transfer your franchise over to our new management group. Oh, and we need you to send us a check for $50,000."

I hung up the phone feeling like I'd been hit by a truck. ANOTHER franchise owner? This was the third time in nine years that my Schaumburg fitness center had been sold. Every time, it required a huge investment of *my* time and money to switch signage, stationery and all other marketing materials to the new brand. Now they wanted *more* money? I knew that phone call was a turning point for me. I had been less-than-thrilled with the support I was getting from the franchiser. I had to make a big change and take a leap into the unknown. The *last* thing I felt was Courage.

Once the shock wore off, I began to realize that this new problem, like so many before in my life, was actually an opportunity in disguise. I had been thinking about making changes to my business for several years now, even studying new techniques I could add to my fitness and life coaching. This latest disruption of the status quo might be just the kick in the pants I needed to go from thinking to doing.

Change happens—get used to it

Most people don't like change, especially change they can't control. For many, it is perceived, consciously or unconsciously, as a threat – no matter how bad their current situation might be. The funny thing is that, as a person, I have always embraced change. As a matter of fact, my current business is *based* on convincing people that they can change—their fitness level, their mental attitude and their overall satisfaction in life. My previous careers in customer service and direct sales also took off because I followed wherever change took me, to new and interesting adventures.

From the very beginning of my fitness business, I knew that exercising the body is not enough. Women came into my studio wanting to lose weight – but one of the biggest challenges many of them faced was their own lack of self-esteem. I knew how they felt: I had been heavy once and losing the weight was an everyday challenge. As I worked on my own body, I saw how much women associated themselves and their self-worth with a number on a scale. (I was guilty of it, too – that's why there is only ONE photograph of me when I was heavy. ONE. I got really good at hiding from cameras.) Losing weight was only part of the answer.

We are so much more than a number

Eventually I became a certified trainer and started my business to help other women overcome their fear of making changes. I studied nutritional counseling and added that to my services. But more than that, I tried to instill in my clients a sense of worth just as they are—I see them as strong and beautiful women who can take on the world. I want them to see themselves that way, too—*before* they lose the weight. I realized that I wasn't just a fitness coach; I needed to be a workout coach, a nutritional coach, a self-esteem coach, a relationship coach, a career coach, a parenting coach – in short, a life coach. All these things are tied together. Women try to be so many things to so many people they often lose sight of themselves. Weight gain is just an outward manifestation of how they feel inside – overwhelmed and selfless. Step one is to help them rediscover their true selves.

As I addressed these emotional issues with my clients, I began to develop my business further to help them along the way. We needed to catch up with the quickly-evolving business of nutrition and fitness. We wanted to give some of the new ideas a whirl! We needed to focus on our clients, the ever-changing social network business world and how to get clients and give them something new. Strategic partners, business apps, mobile-ready websites, new and quicker systems, online materials – the world around us was moving fast. We were not getting the support we needed from the latest franchise owner.

Could we do this for ourselves? Could we get systems in place that are up to date in our fast-paced industry? It took courage to even consider stepping out of the franchise to grow and develop on our own.

Leading the way, making a difference

Over the years, I also realized that my job was not to *force* my clients to make changes, but to inspire them to make changes by leading the way and empowering them to make good choices. So I started to study leadership: how I could become a better leader in my industry, and how I could teach those leadership skills to my clients. I began to study books by the author John Maxwell and soon became a certified John Maxwell Coach, founding member.

The leadership lessons I have learned have helped me immensely. Many of the same principles apply to weight loss, too: recognizing the problems, setting goals and moving ourselves into the position to deal with them. I learned that it's important to always remember your "WHY." With the business struggles I'd been through, I was losing my focus on me, my goals and what I wanted. I had gone from helping people to just surviving all of the changes. But in order to change for positive growth, you have to do it with a purpose. You need your "WHY" out there in front of you all the time, to help you over all the obstacles that get placed in your way. Your "WHY" can give you courage.

To jump or not to jump – that is the question

Which brings us back to me, sitting at my desk, stunned and speechless, having just gotten off the phone with my latest franchisor. There was *no way* I was going to put another $50K into their pockets. What happened to "support?" What happened to "You're in business for yourself, but not by yourself"? Then it hit me: they were banking on me *not* having the guts to walk away and open my own business. They thought they had me between a rock and a hard place.

As people who know me will tell you, I am very determined. I have an obsession with proving that I can do whatever I have been told I *can't* do. And these guys were telling me that I couldn't go it alone. Which is when I knew that I had to.

"You must do that which you think you cannot do."—Eleanor Roosevelt

As of October 1, 2013, my fitness center became Inspire You Healthy. The transformation began. Our goal was to offer a mobile app, two nutrition programs, in-person coaching for one of the nutrition programs, an FDA-approved machine for cellulite reduction, inch loss and body sculpting, and other holistic services to provide an overall support program to help our clients become the people they want to be. The struggles we have seen over the past 10 years led us to develop our new strategies. We wanted to help our clients do more than lose weight: we wanted to help them rediscover themselves, redefine themselves and reach their personal goals, whatever they may be. Our focus was stronger than ever before.

Then I received a certified letter.

During all this time of struggling with my franchise owner, I had been receiving more and more fees tacked on to the rent for my studio. I sat down with numerous people from the landlord's company and walked through what these charges were and how they had accumulated. Each time I sat down with someone, we worked out a solution, and then I'd find out that they were no longer with the company. This happened FIVE times. Finally, the day after Christmas, I received a notice that read, in essence:

"You have five (5) days to pay all outstanding fees or vacate the premises."

Sometimes you win, sometimes you learn.

Sometimes you win, sometimes you learn —I got that from my John Maxwell Leadership training. Finally, I had to admit to myself that I wasn't going to win this one. With a heavy heart, after much soul-searching, consultations with lawyers, other business owners, and my family by my side like always, I closed the doors on my business in the final days of 2013. ("Oh no!" you may be thinking, "I thought this was supposed to be an inspirational story, one full of hope and success!?" So did I. And, in fact, so it is turning out to be.)

It is amazing what I have learned. Things like: you have to have a five-year plan; you must have key checkpoints for assessing the health of your business – these were all things I learned during my John Maxwell training. I had to take responsibility for my own mistakes. When things went wrong, things that were completely out of my control, I focused on things I could change; I was just focused on plowing ahead, working harder, harder and harder.

The most surprising realization has been…I'm okay. I am a personal trainer and Certified John Maxwell Coach. I take with me all the knowledge and power that I gained from 10 years of running my own business. I have people who come up to me on the street and say, "Thank you. You changed my life. You *saved* my life." All of that I bring to my next adventure. I'm still standing, still dreaming, still planning for a brighter future. I feel confident; my business doesn't define who I am. After all the tears and anxiety passed, a wonderful calm came over me. I know this is what I am meant to do. I've even received signs confirming it. The day I left my studio for the last time, I looked down at the snowy parking lot and lying there was a tiny Christmas tree ornament that said simply: "Hope." I picked it up, hugged it to my chest and put it in my pocket. And Hope has been with me ever since.

Somewhere Over the Rainbow

Did taking this step and closing my business mean that I have courage? I'm not sure stubbornness and courage are the same thing. All kidding aside, the answer is yes. I believe courage is the ability to feel fear, be uncertain, not know the outcome – and do it anyway. All of us have it within us. Sometimes we have to have our backs up against the wall to realize it. As the Wizard of Oz told the Cowardly Lion,

*"As for you, my fine friend, you're a victim of disorganized thinking.
You are under the unfortunate delusion that simply because you run
away from danger you have no courage. You're confusing courage with
wisdom. Back where I come from, we have men who are called heroes.
Once a year, they take their fortitude out of moth balls and parade it
down the main street of the city and they have no more courage than
you have."*

I have always loved that quote. It illustrates the fact that being scared
doesn't mean you don't have courage. Sometimes it means you're sane. The
whole point is: no matter how scared you are, no matter how afraid you are of
failing, remember: the only real failure is failing to try.

You can allow change to get the best of you, or you can harness change
and let it help make the best of you. Let it help you make it through the storm
and keep your focus. To conquer your fear, you need a positive attitude; you
need to suck it up, hold your head high and do it anyway. That's courage. You
will find your pot of gold, somewhere over the rainbow.

The choice is simple. It's as clear as can be. Ask yourself, "Will I master
change or will change master me?"

If you are struggling with your weight, your self-esteem or your goals
in life, real courage means asking for help. Ask yourself these questions: What
did you learn from your failures? If you were guaranteed that you could not
fail, what would you do with your life? What do you wish you could change
now? What is your biggest hurdle to achieving your goals? Are you feeling
healthy and strong in your body and mind? If you are interested in making the
most of your time here on Earth, get someone in your corner to help you make
the necessary changes.

Tina Dunn is a certified trainer licensed by the National Training Institute
and the National Strength and Conditioning Association. She is a founding
member on the John Maxwell Team and chapter director for the Dynamic
Professional Women's Network, where she also currently sits on the executive

board. Of all her accomplishments, she is most proud of her family, her 27-year marriage to Allen and her two grown sons, Bradley and Matthew.

"YOITY ~ You Owe It to Yourself" ~ Tina M. Dunn

Tina Dunn

Tina Dunn has a passion for helping others reach their goals. She has spent twenty years in the fitness and wellness industry, transforming lives as a personal trainer and personal growth coach. She owned and managed a weight management and fitness center for 10 years. Additionally, she holds a certificate in accounting, a National Personal Training Institute license, and a National Strength and Conditioning Association certificate, among several other certificates. Tina is Schaumburg's Chapter Director and sits on the Executive Board for the Dynamic Professional Women's Network.

Juggling daily responsibilities isn't easy; over time, many women find themselves at the bottom of that list. Tina has met hundreds of women who have lost sight of themselves and their goals through the day-to-day challenges of being a wife, mother, employee or employer. She knows that, without a structured and practical daily plan, it's easy to be overwhelmed, or even give up.

That's why Tina began studying John Maxwell's proven leadership methods and developed her own 7-step Rainbow Focus program to help women (and men) reach their full potential – not just in weight loss and fitness, but in all areas of their lives. She utilizes elements of the training experience to enhance her clients' everyday productivity, development and decision-making skills, and create a more balanced lifestyle. Today, Tina is available for workshops, seminars and speaking engagements. If you are interested in discovering your passion, developing your future, overcoming your fears and honing your skills, contact Tina Dunn at info@tinamdunn.com

Tina Dunn
Schaumburg, IL
630-474-LADY (5239)
Young Living Oils #1407086
info@tinamdunn.com
www.inspireyouhealthy.com

Nancy Nance

Never Too Late to Get Fit

I grew up in the Chicago suburbs and was one of the kids that was chosen last for every sports game in school. I was the chubby, non-athletic type, hated gym class and would do anything to get out of any type of exercise.

I always struggled with my weight and averaged 150 pounds when I was 10 years old. I started my first diet that year; I remember it well, since I almost passed out on a visit to Sears from not eating. My weight fluctuated during my teen years, but I mostly carried my weight in my abdominal area.

My weight challenge and resistance to exercise continued into adulthood. After my second pregnancy I reached my top weight of 205 pounds. I am only 5'2, so that was a lot of extra weight for my petite frame. Through dieting I was able to drop 80 pounds and keep most of it off for a period of time. I would gain and lose over time and had no desire to exercise.

When I reached 39 years old, my son was looking for his first job and started to work at a gym nearby. He talked me into coming to visit and get a free workout. So I walked into my first aerobics class – with no clue what I was getting myself into. I took a place in the very back corner and set up my equipment. Everyone else seemed to know exactly what they were doing and they were having fun. I was about 20 minutes into class when I thought I was going to die. I ended up leaving that class early, but walked out thinking that even though it was really hard and would be a challenge, I wanted to come back and meet this challenge.

I continued to come back twice a week. I gradually got stronger and my cardio endurance increased. I actually started to look forward to going and met a few people who were very supportive. It was very helpful to know that people would be looking for me if I didn't attend class: it gave me a feeling of accountability to the group.

As I walked to class, I had to pass by the spin classroom. I would pass by and think to myself that those people must be insane for taking that class. A very small part of my brain was thinking that it would be fun to try. After several months, I built up enough courage to take a class. This time I lasted about 25 minutes and ended up having to get off my bike and sit on the floor with my back against the wall. I had worked out too hard and fast, causing my heart rate to go up quickly and I got dizzy. But again I walked out with that small thought telling me that I could conquer this class. I soon added a weekly spin class to my routine.

I normally attended a 5:30 Wednesday night class and one of those nights the instructor didn't show up. The rest of the class asked me to teach that night. I found an old CD on the stereo, put it in and took my place at the front of the class. Secretly, I had been thinking about getting my certification, so this was a perfect time to get a feel for what it was like to lead a class. That night I fell in love with teaching!

I soon got my certification for spin and started to teach the same Wednesday night class that I had been taking in the past. I quickly went from teaching spin to water aerobics, Pilates, boot camp and many other formats. I ended up getting my personal training certification and weight loss and women's fitness specialist certifications.

Even though I was working out, I continued to have a challenge maintaining my weight along with major digestive issues. I've had digestive problems since I was in my 20s but as I got older, they became worse. It began to impact my daily lifestyle and I knew it was time to investigate to see what was going on. I did the medical tests and they determined I had chronic gastritis. I started on different medications to help ease the symptoms. These medications helped for the short term but the symptoms always returned. I would wake up in the morning feeling good, but by 10:00 I would be experiencing major abdominal pain. This was happening daily after I had my snack of wheat crackers, so I gave up wheat and became wheat and gluten free. My stomach issue cleared up a bit and I dropped 30 pounds. While my symptoms lessened, they were not completely gone.

I continued my search to find relief from my digestive issues; I had tests to identify if I had any sensitivities to certain foods. The foods I had major reactions to included wheat/gluten, dairy and yeast. I eliminated these foods from my diet.

At that time, I also discovered products from Orenda International. I started to take the Ultimate Pack, which includes the All in One Female vitamin, O-tropin, Immune™ and Eaze™. Soon after I added these supplements to my diet, my stomach issues began to clear up by about 80%. I was sleeping better, my hot flashes and hormone issues decreased and I continued to drop and stabilize my weight. I was amazed with the results.

I realized that I had to tell others what I had experienced! The passion to help women live a healthier life and feel good about themselves started to drive me to reach out to others. Women underestimate what they can do; they don't think they can change, or they have tried and weren't successful. I decided to combine my passion for fitness with becoming an Orenda anti-aging specialist to empower women to make healthier lifestyle choices.

I work with women who are brand new to exercise or don't like to exercise or want to return to working out. Exercise is more than just trying to fit into a new dress or dropping a few pounds: building our cardiac endurance and lifting weights make us strong and healthier. There is something about being strong that is empowering. Being able to lift grocery bags and walk up the stairs without becoming out of breath gives you a feeling of accomplishment.

Exercise opens up new relationships and adventures. Like-minded people come together, so working out draws you into new friendships. You are more open to trying new things and may find a passion inside you that you would never have discovered if you were not open to new things.

They say that nothing tastes as good as being thin feels, but I'd like to add that nothing feels as great as being strong and fit, no matter what the scale says. It takes work to achieve, but the important thing is to just get started. I hear people say that they will start exercising after they lose weight, when they are not so tired. The truth is that you just have to start. If you keep waiting for a certain time, you will never start.

No matter what your fitness level or if you really don't like to exercise, the important thing is that you start where you are currently. Everything we do is a progression, especially when it comes to taking care of ourselves. People want to change, but it's hard work and trying to make all the changes we need to make at one time can be overwhelming.

Let me tell you Pam's story. She had lost 70 pounds on Weight Watchers®, but reached a plateau. While she had lost the weight, she was not exercising and had very little cardiac endurance. She reluctantly agreed to begin working out and join a health club. We began to work together and at first she needed to make modifications for different exercises in order to be able to do them. Slowly, the modifications were removed and she was able to do the complete exercise. This was not easy but the key thing is she remained consistent. When she didn't feel like working out, she came anyway; when she got tired halfway through, she didn't give up and quit, she finished. As a result of this consistent behavior she became more toned and fit. She feels great and has accomplished fitness goals that she never believed she could. She now works out four to five times a week and it's become part of her lifestyle.

Exercise is a lifestyle choice; it's more than taking classes. It carries over into your daily decisions about what to eat, how you think and what you do. It's unlikely after a morning workout that you will eat a donut or something sugary. If you work out, you begin to take care of yourself in so many other ways.

You also become a role model for those around you, especially if you have children. They do what we do, not what we tell them to do. We become the prime example of how fitness fits into our lives: it can be as simple as taking walks or riding bikes together.

What we put into our bodies really does make a difference. I believe that we are unable to get the full nutrients that we need from the foods that we eat, even if we eat all organic. The preservatives in our food and the toxins that surround us make it impossible for the average individual to get adequate levels of necessary vitamins and minerals.

Earlier in 2013, Orenda released a new weight loss program called Clean, Burn and Shape. This amazing program was developed to clean the body of toxins, preparing the body to lose weight the healthy way. I am now able to add weight loss products to what I offer my clients.

I bring high-quality nutritional support, encouragement, my fitness knowledge and personal experience to each client that I work with. It is so exciting to see the look in a person's eyes when they are able to run their first mile, lift a heavier weight or do a burpee, when just weeks before they would never have thought they could do something like that.

Nancy Nance

Nancy Nance is a certified personal trainer with the National Academy of Sports Medicine and holds certification as Group Instructor with AFAA, TRX Group and Sports Medicine, Spinning Level 3, Total Control Practitioner, Women's Weight Loss and Women's Fitness Specialist and Bender Pilates. She has been in the fitness industry for seventeen years. She currently teaches at Wheaton Sports Center and the Good Samaritan Health and Wellness Center. She empowers men and women to take back their power to live a healthier life by finding exercises and foods that they can enjoy and staying fit. She worked to develop the Healthy Plus Women's program, designed for women who have a BMI of 30+ and limited ability to exercise.

Nancy lives in the Chicago suburbs with her husband, George. She has three grown children and three grandchildren.

Nancy Nance

Orenda International

775 Leslie Lane

Glendale Heights, IL 60139

708-955-4682

Nnance@comcast.net

www.nancynance.com

Mihaela Marcusanu

Journey to Happiness

It takes a baby a long time to walk, and in a similar way, it takes an adult a long time to learn to first hear, then to follow and surrender to the beat of her own drums.

This is my story of traversing the deep dark forests of lost meaning to find my own inner clearings; it is my journey back *home,* back to my true self, hidden under so many heavy layers.

Chapter 1. Who Else Can I Be If I'm No Good?

"It took me a long time not to judge myself through someone else's eyes"

—Sally Field

I was raised in Romania, in a culture that at that time glorified men and demanded that girls and women serve them, listen to them, and know their place in society as a second-class citizen.

To better understand what this meant, my father was copiously mocked by his buddies when my younger sister was born—having two girls made him "less of a man" than his friends who "produced" at least one boy.

For years, I rebelled against this—I asked everybody "why?", "what makes girls inferior?", "please explain it to me". Of course, nobody could… But it continued to haunt me and made me turn into a tomboy—I would wear only pants, never put makeup on, talk only about serious and scientific matters, and hide my feminine side in any way that I could.

Wanting to be daddy's boy and to be worthy of his attention pushed me into studying mathematics (as he was a Ph.D. in Engineering). Doing this ensured that I counted, that I could be admired, and it "saved" me from being (horror!), "a girl".

But the girl in me never "died". I could cover her legs and hide her chest all that I wanted and I could make her spend hours doing math while other kids were playing outside. Her heart was always bursting with passion and sensitivity. She wrote poetry, she loved the sunsets, the grass, the sea, and hugged the trees when nobody was around. She fell in love with life and was always in awe of everything that she saw.

Luckily, pretending to be someone else for the sake of others creates so much inner tension and is so painful, that sooner or later I had to stop. On a deep level, I realized that I needed to start from where I was—to first *accept and embrace myself fully* before I could get to a better place.

Chapter 2. Can I Fly? Let Me Jump Off the Nest and See...

"It takes a lot of courage to release the familiar and seemingly secure, to embrace the new. But there is no real security in what is no longer meaningful. There is more security in the adventurous and exciting, for in movement there is life, and in change there is power."

—Alan Cohen

It was during my senior year in high school and then in college that I decided **to "risk" it to be myself,** as the pressure inside became unbearable. Even though I continued my studies in mathematics (which became part of my identity), I also started sharing more of who I was with others.

I entered and won poetry contests, published my first poetry book, was selected out of 100 students to translate in French by a publishing company, and had a one-year stint in the Philosophy Department.

A beautiful thing happened once I opened up. I started to sense my own power and the strength of this self that I was once denying with all my might. I started feeling proud of being myself and noticed that people around me not only accepted this new me (well, new to them), but even liked me much more.

In August 1997, I felt that it was time to dig deeper into myself. I left Romania and came with a teaching assistantship to study in the United States. I still remember the day that I got here—I felt terrified. I kept asking myself what had I done: why did I leave the familiar ground back home to go to a new continent with two suitcases of my belongings and a few hundred dollars to my name?

Deep down, I knew the answer to this question. I had come to find myself, to expose myself, to challenge myself and to learn who I was beyond my upbringing and my cultural stereotypes.

I was definitely challenged. Two weeks after landing on American soil, I was given a class to teach at the University while working on my graduate studies. That first semester proved to be extremely hard, as I had to adjust to the new culture (especially to the spoken English), to my students, to my own professors and to living independently – which I had never done before.

Intentionally immersing oneself in a totally new environment has great value and I learned a lot about myself from this 'sink or swim' type of experience. The most important thing that emerged was to ***trust myself***—to know that I can make it, that I can fly on my own, and can make my nest wherever I go.

Chapter 3. The Daily Grind: Kids, Job, Marriage, Illness

"Before I went to jail, (...) I was generally busy from 7 A.M. until midnight. I never had time to sit and think."

—Nelson Mandela

After my graduate studies, I worked for 12 years in two major corporations in the insurance industry, half of that time as a manager responsible for leading teams in Research & Development. In the corporate world I learned about leadership, public speaking, politics, managing projects and people.

As a manager of cross-cultural, diverse teams I had the opportunity to coach, train, and empower the people that reported to or worked with me. I loved that aspect of my work and felt a great personal responsibility for "my people".

During this time my husband and I had two wonderful children—and on the outside we probably embodied the American Dream. Underneath appearances though, our marriage was not going very well, and the busyness of a two-income family with small kids offered us the perfect excuse for not facing this fact and dealing with it.

For long periods of time the kids were sick—ear infections, lactose intolerance and intestinal viruses leading to severe dehydration, colds, flus, pneumonia, countless allergies and asthma. Wanting to cure the cause, not the symptoms, I started searching and pouring over books about alternative medicine, nutrition, vitamins, massage, homeopathy, acupuncture, herbs, energy healing, etc.

A big milestone in my personal development was my decision to give birth naturally (without anesthesia) to my second child. This empowered me enormously, especially since he weighed almost ten pounds at birth. From this experience, I learned once again to **trust myself** and to trust my body to do what it needs to do without my analytical brain having to control the process.

Even though I was very busy as a working parent, I never stopped thinking about my life and about my work in the world. I kept feeling a stronger and stronger tug towards being of service and helping others make their lives better.

Chapter 4. This Is Who I Am

"I was once afraid of people saying, "Who does she think she is?" Now

I have the courage to stand and say, "This is who I am."

—Oprah Winfrey

Standing tall within ourselves and in front of the world does not happen overnight—we slowly move upward and reach farther and higher.

A big "reaching" for me happened within a two-year period when I finished a Ph.D. in applied mathematics and published two more books of poetry, while being a full time manager.

I give this example to people I coach to show that *we do have time*—we are actually ***the creators of our time,*** and if we really want something we have the power to *make time for it,* which will get us what we want.

Another "reaching" took the form of surrounding myself with spiritual mentors, coaches, and therapists to gain more clarity into what I wanted to accomplish and into who I was.

One of my dear mentors (who is also a priest) caught me totally off guard once with the question: "if you truly believed that you are the Light of the World, what would you do?" The answer that rushed out of my mouth amazed me: "I would go tell everybody about the ***Light,*** so that people don't suffer anymore but live with joy".

I mulled over this answer for weeks, not knowing what to make of it—I mean, how does one go and "tell" people about the *Light?* And what does one say about it? It didn't make any sense and yet it did…slowly things began to sink in. I took a few coaching classes, and later embarked in a full length coaching program.

One more 'reaching' in my life materialized when I started to meditate daily. This proved to be one of the best things that I could have done, as it decidedly turned my attention inward, helping me face myself squarely.

All this unearthing that happened over a few years led in the end to piecing together the puzzle of truth—the truth about my marriage, about the type of work I was doing in the corporate world, and about my deepest values and inclinations.

It then took two years to finalize a divorce, to heal from it, and to learn to live as a single parent. After that, it took almost another two years to finish training as a life coach, to learn to design and facilitate my own workshops, and to make possible a drastic career change, while holding down a job and running a household.

Chapter 5. Life by Design & By Grace

"Do one thing that scares you every day"

—Eleanor Roosevelt

In August 2013, I made one of the scariest decisions of my life. I left my left-brain corporate position with its security, benefits, and six figure paycheck, in order to have the life that I wanted. It was a life true to myself and in service of the human potential.

Everybody (friends, family and co-workers) counseled me to stay in the job for the obvious reasons: money, health insurance, etc. I thanked them all for their advice and still turned in my resignation as the fear was churning through my body and was strongly pulling me back.

But my heart's voice had been stronger this time. It had summoned me to "be the change I want to see in the world", as Gandhi put it. It had forced me to give my full attention to what was important to me, and to let everything else fall by the side. Following my heart has now become a priority.

Through the years, I also learned that **whenever something scares me to death that's exactly what I need *to do next*—**that's my surest ticket to *the next level.* Whatever brings butterflies in my stomach is what needs healing and mastering, and the only way to do this is to walk straight through the butterflies.

During the time that I spent doing analytical work, I rarely lived the meaning of Kahlil Gibran's quote *"Work is love made visible",* but now I live its truth every day. My work is simply **love** molded into *written* words (through my blog, articles, books) or into *spoken* words (in coaching sessions, happiness workshops/retreats and work/life balance seminars).

When people ask me what I do, I say that I'm in ***the business of changing lives.*** I'm helping people reconnect with their deepest truth, and to live their life out of that place. I inspire people to act despite their fears, which is the only thing that will help them grow and have the life of their dreams. Such a life is very possible, and it is much closer to us than we think - just several actions away. It is the life **we would have already lived if it weren't for fear.**

To open ourselves to the possibilities around us, we can ask: What is it that holds me back? If I didn't have any fears, where, how, and with whom would I be living now—how would my life be different?

May the time come when we boldly pass through the scary gates of fear, only to meet our joy and greatness on the other side. May we lovingly design each of our days and live them with grace, creativity, and with the intention of serving the higher good.

Mihaela Marcusanu

Dr. Mihaela Marcusanu is a Professional Life and Mindfulness Coach who helps extremely busy people slow down and un-burden themselves, thus living lives they can't wait to get up in the morning for. She coaches from the heart using intuition and creativity, with the added benefit of a very diverse life experience and a strong problem solving background.

She offers mindful math sessions in which she helps kids and adults improve their math grades, or prepare for SAT, ACT, Officer Exams, etc. These sessions have the added benefit of incorporating simple mindfulness/meditation techniques that help not only to decrease math and test anxiety, but also to increase focus and attention to the task at hand (leading to better grades in all subjects and better test scores).

Besides coaching, Mihaela offers seminars, workshops, and retreats. She can be reached for inspirational speaking engagements on work/life balance, living a happy and authentic life, and mindfulness (mindful work, mindful life).

Mihaela is the Founder of "Yes to Happiness"—a company with the mission to serve the human potential by being a catalyst for people's growth through self-awareness and self-leadership.

Her blog (at www.mmarcusanu.com), as well as her poetry books, express her own personal and spiritual growth over the years. She is an avid reader, always ready to open the next inspiring book and learn something new to pass on.

Mihaela Marcusanu
Yes to Happiness
1275 Ranchview Ct
Buffalo Grove, IL 60089
224-619-2776
happy@mmarcusanu.com
www.mmarcusanu.com

Jo (Linda) Giovannoni

An Asphalt Angel's® Self-Taught Journey

I think I was born a tomboy. Shortly after I got my driver's license in the late '60s, I was racing my old Chevy at a Chicago-area drag strip. I wasn't setting records (actually I could probably run down the track faster) but I was having a ball!

My high school boyfriend, Fred, gave me a ride on the back of a motorcycle...I was terrified. Fred decided to teach me to ride solo. The motorcycle that was available was a heavy old Harley® with a foot clutch and a tank shifter. When I stopped I had to make sure one foot pushed in the clutch and the other was on the pavement for balance. He taught me on a dead end street. I'd stop and slowly fall over, sort of like the guy on the tricycle on the TV show *Laugh-In.* I hurt my ankle and as he and one of his friends stood laughing I stormed off with my pride hurt more than my ankle.

Fred rented a small dirt bike, or so I thought. I then discovered that he rented two bikes. He screamed for what seemed like forever until I finally threw my leg over the saddle just to shut him up. The smaller bike wasn't intimidating like the Harley® that I had to kick-start while listening to frightening warnings that if not done correctly the strong compression from the motor could kick the pedal back and break my leg. *Oh, goodie.*

This lightweight motorcycle was easy to start and maneuver. We hit the road and suddenly I was riding! I soon learned that you become one with a motorcycle. Your body language determines where the bike goes. I felt connected with nature more than within the confinement of a car. Oh yeah... *I was hooked.* I soon purchased my first motorcycle, a 1968 650cc Triumph

Bonneville®.

In the mid-'70s I became active in ABATE of Illinois, an organization that guards the freedoms and rights of motorcyclists. I wrote a column for the newsletter. My writing skills were not the sharpest, but few were submitted to the newsletter so any articles were welcome. I enjoyed writing about what I love ... motorcycles.

In 1977, I worked as a bartender and one day just quit my job. This was not my nature, and when the reality sunk in, I panicked. While looking for another job, I stopped by the Harley® dealership in Villa Park to pick up a part. During our conversation, the manager said that they had an opening. I took the job. The first day I was nervous but fairly confident that I knew enough about motorcycles to fake it. I soon learned that *I didn't*. When a customer asked for a part, I'd ask what the part did and where it went. This helped me learn more about my new job.

In the late '70s, I started to see a handful of women riders. I met some girls from Rockford and more than 30 years later, I'm still riding with Patty and her husband, Toby. In 1983, a female riding friend, Cris, learned of a women's club, Women in the Wind (W.I.T.W.) in Toledo, Ohio. I was remarried, and the trip to Toledo would be my first out-of-state ride without Rich. Cris and I met with Becky Brown, founder of W.I.T.W., and with her persuasion, we rode home ready to start the 2nd chapter of W.I.T.W. which is now an international organization.

I was president of the Chicago-area chapter and did most of the ride planning. We typed (no computers back then) a one-page newsletter that we shared with Toledo. In 1985, Cris recognized a need for a motorcycle magazine aimed at women riders. We researched, incorporated, started planning our first issue and went to Milwaukee to request permission from Harley-Davidson® to title the magazine *Harley Women*®. We presented our idea to H-D® executives. I remember that they looked at us like we were a couple of quarts low. But H-D® recognized that the female market was growing, so they approved our venture. Our husbands and friends thought it was a passing whim, but after Harley's® approval they finally took us seriously. We named our corporation Asphalt Angels.

I wondered how I'd pull off the journalism and publishing, since I dropped out of high school when my first husband was wounded in Vietnam. Good thing I didn't know I was in way over my head, or I might not have persevered. I'm not implying that I could publish a magazine about gardening, but about my passion, motorcycles, it almost came naturally.

Next we had to learn the ins and outs of publishing. Planning began in Cris's garage and then graduated to the kitchen table. A good friend and graphic artist, Linda Lentini, loved the idea and came onboard. Soon we were using our first computer, an early Apple Macintosh with a monitor so small you could barely see a half page at a time.

The first issue resembled a black and white newsletter containing photos and stories mainly from our chapter of W.I.T.W. We collated and stitched together the first three issues ourselves to save money. Despite our lack of education and experience, the magazine began to grow. It was the first family-oriented magazine aimed at women riders and passenger riders. There were sections like Asphalt Angels Profiles (short stories with photos of female enthusiasts), Tech Tips, Mailbag, Photo Album pages and a Kids Korner section. We never ran low on photos or articles submitted by readers.

There are many aspects to publishing. This high school dropout learned to sell advertising space, became a journalist, reporter, part-time graphic artist, learned about marketing and dealing with the media, worked trade shows and negotiated contracts with Harley-Davidson® and other companies. And, at the end of each day, I emptied the garbage cans. I learned to face my fears and speak in front of groups and on TV and radio interviews. I occasionally co-hosted *Open Road Radio,* a motorcycle talk-radio show created by Gina Woods and based in Chicago.

Through a series of strange events, I literally found a new career that involved my life's passion. I loved the magazine, the people I met and worked with and the path my life was taking.

"Choose a job you love, and you will never have to work a day in your life." —Confucius

New friends at an East Coast Harley® dealership told us to get on a plane because Malcolm Forbes was presenting his friend, Liz Taylor, with a custom Harley®. Okay, so Liz probably never rode the Harley® Sportster® that Forbes had custom painted to reflect her Purple Passion perfume but, man, he was good at promoting a product! He might have put $8,000 (max) into this Harley® and he received coverage from United Press International, Associated Press, German TV, national news stations and magazines. I felt like I was dreaming as I stood on the grounds of Malcolm Forbes' estate in Far Hills, New Jersey. Liz Taylor and Malcolm Forbes, both decked out in bright red, fringed leather jackets, greeted the media. Throughout the years, we went on to meet many Harley®-riding celebrities.

Cris left the company in the early '90s and I continued with the daily struggle to keep it alive. Another girl came aboard to help with the graphic arts. You might have heard of her, Christie Ruffino?! She was a welcome addition and we've been friends ever since. Christie even modeled for advertising photos to promote the Asphalt Angels clothing line. (If you can call four tops a clothing line.)

Many amazing events came about from my venture with *Harley Women*® magazine. In the early '90s, Alice Stone, from Boston, included me as one of five women portrayed in her documentary *"She Lives to Ride"*. I posed on my 1988 Harley® for a motorcycle trading card produced by Skybox. In 1996, I was the fifth woman inducted into the National Motorcycle Hall of Fame for my work promoting women in motorcycling.

Then, as Harley-Davidson's® business boomed, they cut their advertising budget and after several other unforeseen circumstances, I nearly lost the magazine. I had to let my handful of employees go.

"Good judgment comes from experience, and a lot of that comes from bad judgment."—Will Rogers

I bartended part-time because I seldom took a paycheck and there were times I wanted to call it quits after working 80-plus-hour weeks. Then I'd open an envelope and along with a subscription renewal there'd be an extra donation with a note that read *"...your magazine is the reason I began riding and it means so much to me. Please use this extra money for whatever* Harley Women® *magazine needs."* One note read *"...when the magazine arrives, I hide it so I can read it before my husband grabs it."* This homespun magazine meant the world to me and also to my readers. At one point subscribers donated enough to pay the printing bill! Their loyalty inspired me to continue.

Eventually I hired two good friends to help with the daily activity of publishing and putting on events for women enthusiasts. With other friends volunteering their help and readers providing encouragement, I kept the magazine going until 1998 when I had to sell it or see it go under.

I look back and know there were things I could have done differently. I also know that there are many people who are afraid to take a chance in the first place. Instead, they stay in a job that's a daily struggle because they're afraid they will fail if they go on their own. When they look back at their life, I can't help but wonder if they'll think "what if?" I'm not suggesting jumping in head first, but if your passion can be incorporated into your life's work, you owe it to yourself, and your future self, to investigate the prospect.

We learn so much through education and continue to learn from hands-on experience. If your drive is coming from your heart it will be motivating, exciting and will probably take the "work" out of the "job." By the way, I studied hard and received my GED and went on to take a few college courses.

Then, in 2009, life as I knew it changed forever.

After more than four decades of safe riding, a distracted teenage boy turned into my path. Years of riding experience and training from two Experienced Rider Courses kicked in and my reactions probably saved my life. After three surgeries and more physical therapy than I care to remember, I'm better but will have to live with a certain amount of pain.

Terrified of the bills and new at dealing with accident injuries, I immediately contacted the law firm of Hupy and Abraham. For years, I helped distribute the free stickers they print that read "Watch for Motorcycles." I felt that any law office that makes money from (motorcycle) accidents and then spreads the word to help keep riders safe, is a class act. A few years later, Hupy and Abraham asked me to join their firm as an accident investigator. I took the position, leaving my job at a local Harley® dealership, and have never regretted my decision. By the way, they also give away free stickers that read "Watch for Pedestrians" and "Don't Text and Drive."

To date, I've owned one Triumph® and 10 Harleys®. I currently ride a 2012, 103 cubic-inch Heritage® Softail®. I have somewhere around 500,000 miles in the saddle and can't imagine life without a motorcycle.

Do I miss *Harley Women*® magazine? I sure do. It was one of the most significant times in my life and defined who I am today. I do not regret the long hours, sacrifices or financial strain. I put my heart and soul into it and I might have failed to keep the business going, but I succeeded in so many other ways.

I also have the satisfaction of knowing that I didn't sit on the sidelines wondering "what if?"

Harley-Davidson® and Softail® are registered trademarks of Harley Davidson®, Inc.
Bonneville® is a registered trademark of Triumph® Motorcycles, Ltd.

Jo (Linda) Giovannoni

Jo Giovannoni began riding in 1967 in the Chicago suburbs, never dreaming that it would lead to her becoming the 5th woman inducted into the National Motorcycle Hall of Fame.

In the mid-1970s, Jo was very active in motorcycle rights and in 1983 she co-founded the second chapter of Women in the Wind (WITW), now an international group. In 1985, she co-founded *Harley Women® Magazine,* which was created for women motorcycle riders. Jo also started the Queen of the Hill Drag Race, an all-woman all-Harley® drag race held during the Black Hills Motor Classic in Sturgis, S.D.

In 1991, Jo appeared in the film *"She Lives to Ride"* by Alice Stone of Filkela Films in Boston and she was a guest speaker when the film debuted at the Chicago Art Institute. In 1992, *Harley Women® Magazine,* Jo and her former partner were included in the American Motorcycle Association's

Heritage Motorcycle Museum's display on "Women in Motorcycling." Jo also appeared on one of the Harley-Davidson® People collectors cards (similar to baseball cards) produced by Skybox International.

In 2009, Jo's world changed when she was hit by a distracted driver. Her accident led to her current position as an accident investigator for Hupy and Abraham, the creators of the "Watch for Motorcycles" campaign.

Jo (Linda) Giovannoni
Hupy and Abraham
501 N Riverside Dr. Suite 101
Gurnee, IL 60031
847-341-BIKE (2453)
biker1jo@sbcglobal.net
www.hupy.com

Joan Maiden

Go Ahead—Open the Door

"There is always one moment…when the door opens and lets the future in." —Graham Greene

As I approached the door of the gym, I asked myself "What in the world am I doing here?" Little did I know walking through that door would change my life. My world was falling apart. My marriage was failing and my beautiful daughter was slowly starving herself to death. "You need to do something to take care of yourself," my therapist kept insisting. Being overweight and out of shape, joining the gym seemed like a good option.

Eating for two and a family history of obesity made gaining a ton of weight easy. My thirteen-year-old daughter, Mandy, was in the grips of anorexia. I ate to encourage her to eat. My weight ballooned while she got thinner and thinner. When her weight dropped to sixty-five pounds, the doctor said that if she wasn't hospitalized, she would die.

Cradling my little girl in my arms that night, I kept seeing the precious baby that I held in my arms the day she was born, the smiling toddler who charmed everyone and the excited little girl on her first day of school. "What happened—what did I do wrong?" I kept asking myself.

Entering the hospital door the next day with Mandy, and then exiting the same door and leaving her behind, was one of the hardest things that I have ever had to do—but walking through that door saved her life.

Now, pushing open the door to Gold's Gym and stepping inside, little did I know it was the first step to a new life—one I never could have imagined—

never in a million years.

At the gym I met Monica, a personal trainer. Not only was she in great shape, she was the same age as me and had also been overweight. Monica told me that it was time to get into the weight room with the "big boys" and to quit wasting time on the "wimpy weights."

As I started building muscle and losing fat, changes to my body were soon noticeable. I was getting stronger—but not just physically. My self-esteem and self-confidence were also becoming stronger and I found the strength and courage to leave my marriage. I needed to be strong, not just for myself, but for Mandy as well, as she started on the long road of recovery from anorexia.

Mandy started college. I had a good "secure" job and bought a home. Life was all planned out, or so I thought, but something was missing. There was no sense of purpose or passion in my life.

"We must let go of the life we had planned to have the life that is waiting for us." —Joseph Campbell

Standing outside the hospital room door, I thought back over the years and my friendship with JJ. Unlike most kids, I dreaded recess. Being painfully shy, I always felt like an outsider. It was awful when the teacher organized sports and chose captains (who always seemed to be the popular kids) to pick teams. "Please don't let me be chosen last," I would beg inside. Many times, JJ and I were the last two left standing—me, the shy kid who couldn't throw a ball if her life depended on it, and JJ, the fat kid. A lifelong friendship was forged.

Today was JJ's fiftieth birthday. Her weight had increased to the point that she had been in a wheelchair for two years, unable to walk. Her health had also deteriorated and she was now in the hospital.

The doctors and physical therapists gave up on her and told her she would never walk again unaided. They made me SO angry. From what I'd learned at the gym, I knew that new muscle could be built, no matter what a person's age or condition. When JJ returned home, I took her some dumbbells and showed her some exercises. She thought I'd lost my mind, but by Christmas, six months later, she surprised her family by walking unaided.

As teenagers, JJ and I spent a lot of time listening to records. "California Girls" by the Beach Boys was one of her favorites. As she got stronger, she decided it was time to follow that teenage dream and become a "California Girl". It was California or bust! Opening the door and climbing into her van, JJ was following her dream. Little did she know what challenges and opportunities awaited her.

Arriving in California, there were difficult times, but she persevered. And now, unlocking the door to her boutique, JJ thought, "I never would have imagined this—never in a million years." When she headed to California, she never dreamed that she would now be living independently for the first time in years, be just minutes from the beach, have wonderful friends and even find romance—not to mention, own her own business.

One day I was complaining to JJ, as I admit I sometimes do, about how dissatisfied I was with my job.

"So quit," she replied.

"And do what?" I asked.

"Why don't you become a personal trainer?"

Now I knew that JJ had lost her mind.

"You, of all people, know how unathletic I am," I responded. "Besides, I'm over fifty years old. That is just too old to start that kind of career."

"People like me need people like you to help us," was her answer.

Ok, she shamed me into at least finding out what it would take to become a personal trainer. I sent off for the books—and they sat in the box for six months. "I must be crazy to think I can do this," I kept thinking. Finally, dragging the books out of the box, I started studying them, took the personal trainer exam and, to my amazement, passed!

Framing my certificate, I thought, now what? At JJ's urging, I wrote a letter to a gym to see what would happen and was offered a part-time job as a personal trainer. I LOVED it! Helping people build their strength was my life's purpose and passion.

Still working my full-time job and doing personal training part-time, I yearned to train full-time. Eventually, I was offered a full-time personal training job in a city where I knew NO ONE! It was scary. When I called JJ once again, she advised, "If you don't try it, you'll always wonder." She was right. I quit my job, sold my condo and moved.

Turning the doorknob to my new house, I wondered what in the world I was going to do with so much space. The job didn't work out, but I had been led there for a purpose I couldn't yet see.

A doctor called me looking for a trainer to work with an eighty-year-old woman. He encouraged me to start my own personal training business to help people who weren't comfortable going to a gym—older people and those with physical limitations to exercise. It just so happened, my house had the perfect space for a personal gym.

Standing outside the door of the auditorium, my heart filled with pride. Mandy had not only beaten the odds and recovered from anorexia; she was now graduating from college. Having always loved books and words, becoming an editor was the perfect career choice for her. When she was offered a job in San Francisco, she was apprehensive about moving halfway across the country. Repeating JJ's advice to me, I told her, "If you don't try, you'll always wonder." Off she went to California, where she is now happy and successful.

Pushing open the hotel room door in Monterey, California and stepping into the pre-dawn chill, I walked to the starting line of the race while asking myself, "Why am I doing this again?" When Mandy had called me the previous year and asked me to run the Big Sur Half Marathon with her, I reluctantly agreed. Not having run on a regular basis in over twenty-five years, I was apprehensive. When I'd tried running in the past, my knees would hurt for days. Running just wasn't for me, I decided. But I started training, and found, to my surprise, that my knees didn't bother me nearly as much. Having built strength and muscles in my legs gave support to my knees.

Running that first half marathon was tough. However, I told myself that quitting wasn't an option—to just keep putting one foot in front of the other. After crossing the finish line and being presented with my medal, I knew I CAN DO ANYTHING!

Having proven that I could run a half marathon, all thirteen miles, why sign up to do it again this year? Turning sixty was a huge milestone and running the race at sixty was an accomplishment I wanted to achieve. Due to her work and travel schedule, Mandy wasn't going to run the race this year. I would be running on my own and I seriously considered backing out.

Arriving at the starting line as the sun was peeking over the horizon of the bay, the runners' enthusiasm was infectious. Feeling the cool ocean breeze on my face and hearing the waves crashing on the rocks, I decided to just do my best and enjoy the run. Instead of feeling like I was dying, like I did last year, this time I felt really GOOD! Running had even become a form of meditation. Crossing the finish line, I couldn't believe it—I had knocked almost ten minutes off last year's time.

The medals are on my dresser where I can see them every day as a reminder. When encountering challenges and when doubts start to arise— which they have a way of doing—quitting is not an option. All that is necessary is to keep putting one foot in front of the other.

Business and life were good, but once again I was restless inside. Many women facing the challenges of aging are overweight, out of shape and questioning where they will find the strength for what lies ahead. Building strength, I knew, could help these women, as it had helped me and so many of my clients, but how could I convey the message?

Once again, I found myself standing outside a door thinking, "What am I doing here?" Attending my first Engaging Speakers meeting, knowing no one inside, I didn't know what to expect. But it dawned on me that public speaking was the perfect vehicle to deliver the message of strength. The shy kid, too scared to speak up, actually had a talent for public speaking, and I even enjoyed it.

Attending that meeting has opened even more doors. I've made friends, found people willing to give advice and help, and I have been encouraged to start writing my first book. It was through Engaging Speakers that the opportunity to write this chapter presented itself.

Opening the door to Gold's Gym that day not only changed my life, but the life of countless others. It led to other doors opening that I never could have imagined.

What new doors lie ahead? I don't assume to know because through every door life has handed me unexpected surprises. I can't wait to see what's next!

What door are you waiting to open? It may be the door to a gym, a classroom, a meeting, a church, or someone's home. When you get ready to open that door, don't assume you know what's on the other side. You may make new friends and find opportunities, or encounter your life's purpose and uncover your passion. It may even be the first step to a whole new life—one you never could have imagined—never in a million years.

Go ahead—open the door.

"If the door opens, go through it. Always go forwards." —David Soul

"To take the first step in faith, you don't have to see the whole staircase; just the first step." —Martin Luther King, Jr.

Joan Maiden

Based on the real transformations that have taken place in Joan's life, she founded MPower Coaching, which is dedicated to helping others transform their lives, make positive changes and realize their dreams. For the past decade, Joan has helped numerous clients regain mobility, quality of life and renewed health and fitness.

Joan teaches that disease and disability do not have to be a natural part of aging. Much of the frailty associated with aging is simply caused by muscle loss, and new muscle can be rebuilt at any age. Building strength can turn the body from a liability to an asset. Your body is the dwelling for the soul—and it deserves a strong, healthy temple.

MPower Coaching stands for **MY** Power. *It's time to take back your personal power.*

Joan has professional certifications in the following areas of expertise:

- Professional Member, *Engaging Speakers*

- Certified Healthy Behaviors Coach, *Cooper Institute, Dallas, Texas*

- Certified Personal Trainer, *American Council on Exercise*

- Certified Lifestyle Weight Management Counselor, *American Council on Exercise*

- Certified Trainer, Balance, Stability, Mobility and Conditioning for the 50+ Adult, *SCW*

Joan Maiden
MPower Coaching, Inc.
3609 Guilford Rd.
Rockford, IL 61107
217-898-3391
joan@maidenpower.com
www.maidenpower.com

Volume III

Now interviewing authors for our next edition,
scheduled to be released late 2014.

www.overcomingmediocrityteam.com